YOU'RE

CHANGE THE WAY

YOU FEEL ABOUT YOURSELF

WORTH

BY DISCOVERING

HOW JESUS FEELS ABOUT YOU

IT!

DANIELLE BEAN

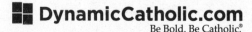

DynamicCatholic.com
Be Bold. Be Catholic.®

Cover design: Connie Gabbert

ISBN: 978-1-942611-74-5 (hardcover)
ISBN: 978-1-942611-75-2 (softcover)

Library of Congress Cataloging-in-Publication Data

Names: Bean, Danielle, author.
Title: You're worth it! : change how you feel about yourself by discovering how Jesus feels about you / Danielle Bean.
Description: North Palm Beach, FL : Beacon Pub., 2016.
Identifiers: LCCN 2016015140 (print) | LCCN 2016016069 (ebook) | ISBN 9781942611745 (hardcover) | ISBN 9781942611752 (softcover) | ISBN 9781942611769 (ebook)
Subjects: LCSH: Christian women--Religious life. | Self-perception in women--Religious aspects. | Self-perception--Religious aspects--Christianity.
Classification: LCC BV4527. B3925 2016 (print) | LCC BV4527 (ebook) | DDC
248.8/43--dc23

Dynamic Catholic® and Be Bold. Be Catholic.® and The Best Version of Yourself® are registered trademarks of The Dynamic Catholic Institute.

For more information on this title or other books and CDs available through the Dynamic Catholic Book Program, please visit www.DynamicCatholic.com.

The Dynamic Catholic Institute
5081 Olympic Blvd • Erlanger • Kentucky • 41018
Phone: 1–859–980–7900
Email: info@DynamicCatholic.com

Printed in the United States of America

To Jesus, whom I love in my own small and imperfect way. I wrote this book with you and for you, praying to touch the hearts of those who would read it. These words are for you. This book is for you. Your will be done.

TABLE *of* CONTENTS

AN INVITATION

We were only Facebook friends. Our children played many of the same sports and attended school together, so we talked sometimes in real life, but we weren't close. More like acquaintances, really.

But all that changed the day I sat through a school awards assembly with her seated nearby. Her youngest child whimpered on her lap while her toddler climbed up and down the folding chairs, his shoes clanging noisily against the metal seats. I saw her face grow red as she shushed them, soothed them, and begged them to be quiet before finally cutting her losses, packing up their bags, coats, and board books, and heading to the back of the room. There she stood, balancing the baby on her hip and chasing the toddler, who repeatedly bolted for the fire exits.

When the assembly finally ended, I looked up and saw her standing nearby, looking thoroughly depleted. As I passed, I paused to give her a smile. "That was a rough time, but you did great!" I commented, trying to encourage her. I went to give her a quick hug and was surprised to find that she did not let go. Because she was crying so hard.

"My life is falling apart," she sobbed onto my shoulder. "I can't do this anymore."

SHARING OUR HEARTS

The two of us retreated to a corner, and she spilled what was on her heart. The tears weren't about her children's behavior at all. They were about a husband who was cold, distant, and obsessed with work, a car repair bill she couldn't afford to pay, her mom's abnormal mammogram, and some good old-fashioned exhaustion. We talked for an hour—and became friends for life.

"I'm so embarrassed," she texted me later. "I don't usually fall apart like that."

Of course she doesn't. None of us do. We're all too busy putting on a brave face, even on the worst of days and through the hardest of times, to let any weakness show.

"I am honored," I texted back, "that you would share your heart with me."

I truly was. I truly am. Each time a sister or friend or even a stranger opens her heart to me, I am humbly aware of what a privilege it is to share that moment. It's not something we women take lightly.

"I hate my body," a woman at the gym might want to confess.

"I'm afraid my boyfriend just wants sex and will never marry me," a woman in the ladies' room might want to say.

"My grown son is no longer talking to me," a mom in the church parking lot might want to admit.

But we don't say these things. We don't share them because we are ashamed, and they are hard to admit. Each time we let ourselves be vulnerable and share our hurts and our hearts, though, we women find out that we are not alone, and we are instantly connected—friends and sisters forever. We don't do that often enough.

I recently hosted a large party at my house and did what was typical for me. I rushed about, doing all the "important" things and refusing help from anyone who offered. One of my guests stopped me as I headed toward the kitchen with a stack of dishes. "Let me help you," she offered.

"Oh, no!" I said, grinning at her. "I've got this!"

My friend held my arm to gain my attention. "Let me be a *friend* to you," she said gently.

Oh. That. That friend thing requires honesty, vulnerability, and admitting we can't do it all alone. It's not always easy, and yet it's so empowering when we do.

BEING VULNERABLE

I am working on being vulnerable, and in this book I hope to encourage you to do the same. It's only when we open ourselves up, when we share our hearts, that we can truly be known and loved. That we can truly be our best selves. That we can fully reach our potential.

And even more precious than being able to share your heart with a human friend is the possibility of friendship with

Jesus. Every person reading these lines right now is loved by Jesus with a personal, infinite, irreplaceable love. He loves each of us as if there were only one of us. And he wants to be closer to us than any friend on earth could ever be.

Do you find that hard to believe? I sometimes do. We can talk about Jesus, and read about Jesus, but is he real? Does he feel real to you? Do you feel like you can know him and he can know you? Do you consider him a friend—someone you can trust with your deepest thoughts and feelings? Someone who can *change your life?*

Especially if you are hurting—and so many of us are wounded in this world—Jesus can feel like a nice idea, a pretty statue, or a storybook character from a long time ago, but certainly not someone we can have a real relationship with. Not someone who has relevance and matters in our lives today. But you are reading this book for a reason. Perhaps someone gave it to you, or perhaps you picked it up yourself, intrigued by an invitation to experience something life changing. We all want to feel blessed, to feel loved and cherished. We women live out our lives giving love and seeking it in return. A deep-seated need for love is why so many of us make compromises with our bodies and in our relationships. We think that if we just do the right things, and say the right things, and look the right way, at last we will be loved. We think this is the way to be fulfilled.

We are seeking something that will fill us, satisfy us, and make us feel known, wanted, and loved. We want to do our best; we want to look and feel our best; we want to be our best. We will do anything to have that.

LET HIM IN

Jesus is real, he is fully human, and he loves each of us in a deeply personal way. He wants to make sure we become the person God created us to be. He knows and loves the real you—and he knows that's the *best* you. But I know we can hear these words and want to believe them, and yet some part of us still rejects the idea of Jesus' love. Maybe because we think we need to be independent and tough, or maybe because deep down, we fear we are unworthy of love. The thing is, though, none of us can earn Jesus' love. He doesn't love us for what we do or say or wear or look like. He loves each of us for who we *are*. To be truly loved, we just need to be.

Whatever your reason for holding back, my goal in these pages is to help you open your heart and let go of fear and insecurity. My hope is that you'll begin to know Jesus, develop a friendship with him, and let him change the perceptions you have about yourself.

Because you're worth it.

Because Jesus *does* want to change the way you see yourself. He wants to love, strengthen, heal, affirm, hear, fulfill, and nurture you. All you have to do is let him. In this book, we'll cover seven ways that Jesus can change your life.

WOMEN WHO KNOW JESUS

How possible is it to really know Jesus in our materialistic world, centuries after he lived on earth? We are physical creatures, after all, and we believe in things that we can see, hear, smell, and touch. Jesus is not present to us in those ways today. How well can any of us really know him?

The women we meet in the Bible are real, though, and they knew Jesus. They saw him, heard him, and experienced his healing touch. We women today can look to our biblical sisters who have gone before us, and from their experiences we can learn more about Jesus and the ways he wants to change our lives. Jesus was real to them, and he is real to us today, and they can help us see that.

The New Testament is filled with an astonishing variety of women. They are all uniquely beautiful, sinful, struggling, seeking, suffering, faithful, wounded, broken, and strong, and their real stories detail the good things—mercy and forgiveness, healing and love—that Jesus longs for each of us to experience. In each chapter of this book, we will consider the personal stories of women who knew Jesus in real life, and we'll discover the secrets their lives reveal.

At the end of each chapter, we will also meet modern-day women who have experienced the life-changing love of Jesus in deeply personal ways. While their lives are vastly different from those of the women of the Bible, they all have at least one thing in common: a real relationship with Jesus.

If you're ready to consider how Jesus might change the

way you think about yourself, if you're willing to explore how he can transform your life, I invite you to join me in a journey of possibility.

Well, what are we waiting for? Let's get started.

CHAPTER ONE

YOU ARE LOVED

"As the Father has loved me, so have I loved you;
abide in my love."

(JOHN 15:9)

He was the cute boy we all giggled about. I was a junior in high school, and my friends and I were participating in a government education weekend at the statehouse. We were too shy to talk to him, but we watched from a distance and gave him a nickname based on his wardrobe: Red Tie Guy. So I was beyond flattered when on the last afternoon Red Tie Guy crossed the room to talk with me. To flirt with me. And to ask me out for the next weekend.

Of course I said yes. And all my girlfriends swooned.

After going out for burgers and watching a movie, we ended up at his house, in his room, with his parents gone for the evening. And then suddenly he was grabbing at me. Pulling at my shirt. Grasping at my jeans. His mouth was on my neck and his hands were all over me.

It was gross. It was scary. I pushed him away. Red Tie Guy grew angry and pushed back. And he said things, terrible things I will never repeat, about who I was and what I was good for. His words and actions told me I was useless, a throwaway.

I am grateful to have parents who taught me to know better than that. I pushed him away one last time, hard. And then, shaking all over, I called home, and waited outside.

When my dad came to pick me up, he did not notice that my T-shirt was torn. He did ask me if everything was OK, and I told him it was. I was fine, really I was, except I was shaken to the core because I never would have guessed that someone I liked, someone I thought liked me, could suddenly turn into someone so violent and hateful.

Does that sound naive? I suppose it does, but it was true. I did not know a person would ever use another person that way. That's a beautiful testament to my blissful childhood and a sad coming-of-age story all at once, isn't it?

Many times since that night, though, and especially since becoming a mom to daughters myself, I have paused to wonder: *What if I didn't know better? What if I took that boy at his word when he told me what I was good for?* It breaks my heart to think of it, but his words about my worthlessness are what so many girls hear and believe—and they grow up to be wounded women.

Have you heard words like that? Did you believe them? Do you still? Do you know—can you possibly know—how untrue they are? You might not have a Red Tie Guy in your past, but you may have experienced something that made you feel the same way. Maybe you have been personally rejected in a romantic relationship, or a family member abused you and made you feel worthless. Whatever anyone else in the world has told you about who you are and what you are worth, Jesus has something new to say.

He wants to tell you that you are beautiful. You are unique, you are precious, you are blessed, and you are loved. Jesus wants to love you with a deep, personal, soul-satisfying love. Will you believe him? Will you let him?

Not yet? That's OK. These things take time. Let's begin by meeting another woman who once felt used up and worthless, and find out what she can tell us about Jesus. She knows Jesus, you see, because she met him one day at a well.

ENCOUNTER AT THE WELL

It was midday and Jesus, who was traveling through Samaria on his way to Galilee, stopped to rest at a well in the tiny town of Sychar. He had to go out of his way to get to this well, and it was not just any well; it was the well of Jacob. For generations, this source of life-giving fresh water had been seen as a sign of God's blessing upon Jacob and the Jewish people.

Many Jews at the time avoided entering the foreign land of Samaria. They believed that years of intermarriage among races and the worship of false gods had rendered the land of Samaria and its people unclean. Though the most direct route from Jerusalem to Galilee was straight through Samaria, it was common for Jews at the time to add many miles to their travels in an effort to avoid passing through the area and encountering its "unsavory" inhabitants.

Jesus, however, was unafraid of Samaria and the Samaritans. He was not concerned with "uncleanliness" or the scandal his association with "undesirable" people and places might cause among his fellow Jews. Jesus did not care about being politically correct. There, in the middle of the day, he stopped to rest at Jacob's Well and engaged a local woman in conversation. The almost-casual way that Scripture introduces this story belies the deeper meaning behind what seems like a chance encounter and conversation.

> So he came to a city of Samaria, called Sychar, near the field that Jacob gave to his son Joseph. Jacob's well was there, and so Jesus, wearied as he was with his journey, sat down beside the well. It was about the sixth hour. There came a woman of Samaria to draw water. Jesus said to her, "Give me a drink." For his disciples had gone away into the city to buy food. (John 4:5–8)

EVERY WOMAN

Some of us are familiar with the story of the woman at the well whom Jesus engaged in conversation, but one thing none of us know is her name. The Bible mentions many individuals by name, even some who played small and much less significant roles, but the Samaritan woman who met Jesus at the well goes unnamed.

There are no accidents in the Bible; every mention and every omission has meaning. So what are we to make of the fact that this woman, who spoke at length with Jesus about matters of the utmost significance, is not mentioned by name?

We might draw from her anonymity that the story told in this passage, the conversation recorded here, is not this woman's story alone, but one that belongs to every one of us. The intimate encounter with Jesus described here is one that each of us is called to—especially women, because it is also not accidental that instead of referring to her by name, over and over again, the Bible refers to her as "the woman." Nameless through the ages, the woman at the well is every woman.

She is me. She is you. We are present, in this story, with Jesus.

BREAKING THROUGH

One of the most striking facts about the conversation between Jesus and the woman at the well is the fact that it happened at all. As far as reputable Jews at the time were concerned, such a conversation was scandalous in three serious ways. First of all, Jesus was speaking to a woman. This broke a social taboo at the time, as Jewish men typically did not address women in public.

The second strike was that the woman was Samaritan. As previously noted, the Jews went to great lengths to avoid interaction with these "unclean," racially different people who worshipped false gods.

And finally, the woman at the well was a sinner. The fact that she was drawing water from the well at midday instead of early in the morning, when most other women performed this task in order to avoid the heat, indicates that her sinful series of marriages had made her an outcast. She avoided social interactions, even with her own people.

But Jesus did not care about any of that. Ignoring social, racial, and religious barriers, he looked into the eyes of the woman at the well, spoke directly to her, and touched her heart. This is because Jesus knows no barriers. He pursues a personal relationship with each of us, in spite of human obstacles.

We might think our past stands in the way of us experiencing Jesus' love. We put labels on ourselves and believe that they are obstacles to love. "I'm an addict," we might say, or "I've had an abortion." "I'm divorced," or "I have failed my children."

But Jesus exists in the present, and he is not concerned with labels and restrictions. He passes through every obstacle we throw in his path, all the "shouldn'ts" and "can'ts" we might think of, and waits to meet us at the well.

WHERE JESUS MEETS US

I love that, in this story, the woman encountered Jesus when she was in the midst of her daily routine. There are few things more mundane than the kind of work we women do to provide food and drink for our families. Meal planning, grocery shopping, cooking, and dishwashing are not glamorous jobs, and yet they are the necessities of daily living, more often than not performed by women—wives, mothers, sisters, and daughters—in every age and every culture. The Samaritan woman in this story was going to the well to draw a daily portion of water for her family when she bumped into Jesus. He was waiting there patiently, in the path of her daily routine, right where he knew she would be.

Do you see? We don't have to get fancy to meet Jesus. On your knees in a church is a great way to connect with God, but it's not the only way. In fact, it's probably not the first place most of us encounter God in a meaningful way. Jesus knows each of us and loves each of us in a uniquely intimate way, right where we are. He knows every tiny detail of our daily lives, waits for us in those everyday moments, and longs for us to seek him and meet him there.

A HUMAN GOD

"Give me a drink," Jesus said to the woman at the well.

The Bible tells us Jesus was traveling and was tired and thirsty. When I think of these words, I am amazed by their simplicity. Few things connect us more directly with the frailty of our humanity than experiencing physical needs when we travel.

Whenever I travel, I am struck by the fact that the human beings on an airplane, in a restaurant, or checking into a hotel are concerned about some pretty simple stuff. You might be a rocket scientist, a great theologian, or a neurosurgeon, but at the end of the day, you have a body that requires care. On the road and away from the comforts of our homes and beds, we must concern ourselves with the basics. Where will we eat, where will we sleep, and is there a bathroom nearby? Jesus had to concern himself with these things, too.

Jesus is both fully God and fully human, a mystery that is difficult for us to understand, and yet I like to imagine what that might have been like during his time on earth. Jesus grew weary on the road. The Creator of the universe grew tired of travel and needed a drink of water. This is an extraordinary thing to ponder.

Imagine the love of an all-powerful God who longs to connect with us tiny humans so much that he is willing to take on humble human form in order to do so. The story of the woman at the well highlights the fact that Jesus, through his humanity, aims to do exactly that. God could speak to us from a cloud of thunder in the sky. Jesus could have gotten the Samaritan woman's attention with a miraculous healing or a laser light show, but he chose not to be flashy.

"Give me a drink," he said.

Hospitality is a beautiful gift women have in particular. We notice and care for others' needs, and we excel at making people feel welcome. Knowing this, Jesus initiated his connection with the woman at the well in the most basic of human ways—by asking for a drink of water. He longs to connect with each of us through our shared humanity as well.

And he wants to connect with us in the most basic of ways. He was thirsty. We understand thirsty. Just like the woman at the well, we are quick to help others who are thirsty. As God, Jesus has a right to everything we are and everything we own, but he doesn't begin a conversation by asking for all that we have. He asks for a drink of water. Out of love, he humbly embraced his humanity and asked the woman at the well to make one small move in his direction. He asked for a drink.

A GOD WHO KNOWS US

The Samaritan woman was confused by Jesus' request. Didn't he know the social taboos he was breaking? Wasn't he afraid to speak to a woman, and to share a drinking vessel with not just a Samaritan, but a sinful one at that?

"How is it that you, a Jew, ask a drink of me, a woman of Samaria?" (John 4:9).

And that is when Jesus told her about eternal life: "Every one who drinks of this water will thirst again, but whoever drinks of the water that I shall give him will never thirst; the water that I shall give him will become in him a spring of water welling up to eternal life" (John 4:13–14).

The woman was intrigued. She must have known by that point that Jesus was no ordinary man, and she had realized that the water he spoke of was no ordinary water satisfying ordinary thirst. She was thirsty, in many ways, in her life.

We all are, and Jesus knows this. What are you thirsty for?

When the woman at the well asked Jesus to give her the water he spoke of, though, he replied in a way that might have made her uncomfortable: "Go, call your husband, and come here" (John 4:16).

One problem, though: She didn't have a husband. Or rather, she'd had many "husbands"; she wasn't sure why Jesus was asking this. When she replied that she didn't have a husband, he went on: "You are right in saying, 'I have no husband'; for you have had five husbands, and he whom you now have is not your husband; this you said truly" (John 4:17–18).

Imagine having a chance encounter with a stranger who just happens to know everything about you—even your most shameful sins and secrets. Imagine meeting a stranger who speaks to you candidly and yet kindly about intimate details of your life you have not shared with him. The woman's heart must have been racing. Her mind must have been spinning. *Who is this man? How does he know these things? How can he speak so frankly about these things we never speak of?*

A woman who has had five husbands has to know a thing or two about human relationships. No woman can cycle through five marriages without meeting up with a Red Tie Guy or two, without experiencing heartbreak and failure, and without winding up feeling used up, burned out, and tossed aside. This woman's past was a source of shame—and so was her current relationship with a man she was not married to. Even the Samaritans had a sexual moral code they were expected to live by, and this woman's personal life was a living violation of it.

It is important to note that Jesus did not deny the woman's sin, and he didn't ignore it, either. He spoke about it openly. Especially when it comes to our own sins and guilt, the truth can be very hard to hear, and yet it is essential to our forgiveness and healing. We need to know the wounds caused by our sins in order to be healed from them.

Sometimes the most painful part of sin is its secrecy. Deep and hurtful shame can come from hiding our past, pretending to be something we feel we are not, and denying the real and painful consequences of sin. There is a saying inside many 12-step programs: "You are only as sick as your secrets." So true! Healing comes with the truth.

With Jesus, there are no secrets. Just as with the Samaritan woman, Jesus sees us as we are and loves us anyway. We are daughters of God, and therefore we are worthy of love, despite our sins. The woman at the well experienced love and healing through Jesus' acknowledgment of the truth, and she was so amazed by this blessing that she ran off to tell others in her town about him, leaving her water jar behind. "Come, see a man who told me all that I ever did," she breathlessly told them (John 4:29).

She no longer hid out of guilt and shame. She talked about "everything I have done" without shame because Jesus, who saw her as she was, offered her the gift of eternal life and made her new. Not in spite of her sinfulness, but because of it, he offered her the gift of peace, healing, and forgiveness that can only come from him. After years of seeing herself as an outcast and living with a less-than-positive self-image, she now burst forth with a joy that invited others to meet him.

WHO IS JESUS?

In the course of their conversation, the woman at the well became increasingly convinced that Jesus was the one the Jews had been waiting for. It would have taken guts to ask him outright, so she sidestepped the question a bit by saying, "I know that Messiah is coming (he who is called Christ); when he comes, he will show us all things" (John 4:25).

But Jesus answered her directly: "I who speak to you am he" (John 4:26).

This direct confession of Jesus' identity is unique in the Bible. With his own disciples, he was sometimes frustratingly vague about his identity and purpose, but when this foreign woman asked a sideways question, he gave her the whole truth without obscurity or hesitation.

Jesus admitted that he was the Messiah, the one the Jews had been waiting for, the one who would come to love them, heal them, and save them from their sins. This confession was nothing short of astonishing, as much for its meaning as for the person to whom he made it. Jesus chose to reveal himself not to dignitaries or high priests, not to rich men or important people, but to a "nobody"—a sinful foreign woman in a small town who happened to be drawing water from a well.

This simple truth gives us great hope, as it underscores the fact that Jesus will give every one of us, even the smallest and most sinful of human beings, everything we ask of him. If you ask him for the truth, he will not deny you. If you ask to know him, he will reveal himself to you in amazing ways. If you ask him to make his love real to you, he will do so.

But are you asking?

The woman at the well calls to us still. "Come, see a man," she shouts, "who told me all that I ever did."

Come, see a man who breaks through all barriers in his drive to reach us, connect with us, and love us intimately. Come, see a man who approaches us where we are, who waits patiently in the everyday moments and mundane details of our daily lives. Come, see a man who shares our humanity and longs to connect with us through it. Come, see a man who knows everything about us—even our deepest, darkest, most sinful secrets—offers us the gift of forgiveness, and forever changes the way we view ourselves. Come, see a man who knows the truth, speaks the truth, and will not deny us any good thing we ask from him.

Come, see a man. Come, meet Jesus. Will you come?

IN PERSON
FINDING FORGIVENESS AND PEACE

Chaunie was a "good girl"—an A-student in Catholic school, a cheerful daughter, and a pro-life volunteer. In college, she earned a full-tuition scholarship, had a longtime boyfriend she loved, and landed a prized internship in Washington, D.C.

"I was on top of the world," she recalls. Imagine her surprise, then, when after weeks of feeling exhausted and ill, she finally took a pregnancy test and it was positive.

In her heart, Chaunie knew that being sexually active with her boyfriend did not align with her Catholic faith and her image as a "good girl," but she never imagined it would catch up to her in quite this way. This was the sort of thing that happened to other people.

Chaunie's family got over their shock and did their best to help her make plans to complete school and earn her degree. Her boyfriend proposed, she said yes, and so Chaunie found herself a young woman in her senior year of college, planning a wedding and preparing to become a mom.

But she was not at all prepared to become a mom. She was living in a run-down apartment with a hodgepodge of hand-me-down furniture, still returning to her parents' house each weekend to do laundry. But more than monetary or housing concerns, Chaunie had spiritual and emotional obstacles she needed to overcome.

"In my mind, I was a good person who did something bad," she says, "and that made me feel that somehow I did not deserve anything good anymore."

Looking back now, she realizes that all of her self-worth before and during her pregnancy was caught up in being "good." She felt that she earned the love of God (and others) through her accomplishments and good behavior. So when she failed at being good she felt unworthy of all love and blessing.

"I had sinned," she says, "and I could not reconcile my sin with God's goodness. I could not accept that something good could ever come from something bad."

Even as she planned a wedding to take place over Christmas break of her senior year, Chaunie knew she could not enter into marriage and motherhood feeling the way she did about her circumstances. "I was struggling so much personally and spiritually. I didn't want to get married until I could accept myself and my baby."

Completely closed off, she did not even feel capable of praying. And that was when it happened. Chaunie could not come to Jesus, so he came to her.

She was sitting on a borrowed couch in front of the fireplace in her dingy apartment when she was startled to suddenly feel God's presence in a way she never had before.

"I am not one of those people who walks around saying that God spoke to me," she says with a laugh, "but the presence I felt in that moment was real, and it was God. He was there in the room with me, and he was saying, 'It's OK.' Such a peace overcame me. I saw that everything comes down to love. I could love my baby, and I could bond with her. I could be her mom—the best mom I could be."

After that moment, Chaunie's life was still challenging in many ways, but something fundamental had changed. "That was a huge shift in my personal and spiritual life," she says. "Before I was so focused on rules and being what looked like a 'good girl,' but after that I learned to become more forgiving of myself and others. I learned that everyone needs forgiveness."

Chaunie has not had any more dramatic encounters with Christ since that moment on the couch during her senior year, but she acknowledges that her relationship with God has shifted in powerful ways. She let go of the shame and guilt that kept her from approaching God, and even more important, she learned to stop thinking of love as something that must be earned.

"Especially now that I am a mom, I can see that there is nothing my children can do that would ever make me stop loving them. You don't have to do X, Y, or Z for God to love you. It's a gift. He loves you as you are, for no reason at all."

JESUS IS WITH YOU, TOO

Chaunie was not expecting to find Jesus the way she did, the Samaritan woman was not expecting to meet Jesus at the well, and perhaps you are not expecting to meet with him anytime soon either. But he is planning to meet you. Just as he has done with others, he is waiting in your path. He might be closer than you think.

I remember one day as a new mom years ago when I went shopping at Walmart with my toddler daughter. I did not want to let her out of the shopping cart, but she begged to be free to walk on her own, and eventually I relented. I continued shopping while she walked alongside, holding on to my pant leg. After a few moments of this, I suddenly realized I no longer felt her tiny grip on my leg. I looked down, and not seeing her, I completely panicked.

Where was my daughter? I looked wildly in all directions and called out her name. Fear rose in my chest as I called for her louder still. Where could she be? I made my way down nearby aisles but still did not see her until at last she answered my panicked cries with a small "Mama?" There she stood, right at my feet, holding on to my other leg. She was so close I did not see her.

And that's where Jesus is, too. When we don't think he is near us, when we mistakenly believe that he does not care about our lives, he is waiting right there beside us. Take a moment and see if you can feel his presence. Don't look for him in faraway places. Look for him right where you are, in your own heart. He is waiting there.

Jesus wants nothing more than to connect with us through our shared humanity. He who knows everything about each of us, even our darkest and most shameful secret sins, loves each of us intimately and uniquely. "Give me a drink," he might say, to begin the conversation, but he doesn't really want a drink. He wants to connect with us. Jesus longs to love us, forgive us, and finally to satisfy our own thirst with his saving gift of love and forgiveness. He wants to give you his best so you can be your very best—a shining example of grace and mercy for those who need it most.

Will we allow him to meet us and share with him our deepest hopes and longings? Will we open our hearts and let him see our fear, guilt, and shame? Will we show him our deepest wounds and let him heal them? We are all thirsty. Will we drink?

If you feel ready, open you heart now, just a tiny bit, and pray these words with me:

Here I am, Jesus. I want to know who you are, but I hold back sometimes out of fear. Hurting inside, I hide behind other people's words and labels, and my own secrets and past. But I know you are with me now, in this moment, and that you are speaking to me. Open my ears to hear your voice. Open my heart to see you, know you, and feel loved by you. Open my eyes to see myself the way you see me. I want to be loved. Amen.

CHAPTER TWO

YOU ARE STRONG

*"For human beings this is impossible,
but for God all things are possible."*

(MATTHEW 19:26, NAB)

Years ago, shortly after our third child, Ambrose, was born,
God kicked me in the teeth.

Well, he probably wouldn't say he did that, but it sure felt
that way to me at the time. I was a young mom. Dan and I had
married straight out of college and welcomed our first three
babies in as many years. After blessedly uneventful pregnan-
cies and healthy babies, however, the health of our sweet
newborn son was a source of constant anxiety.

Ambrose had breathing and digestion issues that went
undiagnosed for many stressful months. By the time he was
seven months old and the doctors finally ordered the right
tests, he was diagnosed with cystic fibrosis, a genetic illness
with no cure. At first, it was a great relief to have a name for
what was making him so sick and to gain access to treatments
and medications that helped him thrive.

Soon after his diagnosis, however, reality set in, and I

found myself lying awake at night, thinking of my son's uncertain future, worrying about potential future children, and wrestling with the feeling of being betrayed by a God I trusted.

I had little faith.

I was a Rosary-praying, Mass-attending woman of little faith. Before any of this, I would have told you I was a faith-filled person, and I certainly would have looked the part, but the challenge of my son's illness laid bare an ugly truth: I had faith when it felt good. I had faith when God held up his part of my unspoken deal and life went along just as I planned it. I had faith when I could pick and choose the kinds of sacrifices I would make.

During that difficult time, I remember going to church, kneeling before the crucifix, looking at Jesus on the cross, and having nothing to say. This was a foreign feeling. I always had prayers to say—gratitude to offer, petitions to make, and praise to give. But now I had nothing.

I was spent. I was angry. I was empty.

And it was there, in the silence of those struggling moments, that I first began to know something about Jesus: When it comes to having a real relationship with him, it's OK to bring nothing but yourself. We don't need to bring anything more than ourselves because we are all that he wants. Jesus longs for us, waits for us, beckons for us to come closer, and makes no demands of us beyond our presence.

"Come to me," he says (Matthew 11:28), and this is all we need to grow closer to Jesus. Come to him, even during, or especially during those times when our faith fails us and we have no words left to pray. It is there, in the midst of our silent struggle, that Jesus fills our emptiness, softens our hardness, and strengthens our weakness. It is there that we find our faith and it can begin to grow.

Some of the women who met Jesus during his time on earth had great faith. Others, like me, did not know just how small their faith was until it was tested, but Jesus was patient, and he loved them despite their weakness. Let's meet some of these women now, and find out what their faith, their words, their actions, and their struggles might teach us today.

MARTHA, MARTHA

You know Martha, don't you? Every woman knows Martha, I think, because every woman *is* Martha at some point in her life.

Martha, Mary, and Lazarus were grown siblings who lived together in Bethany, just two miles outside Jerusalem. In the Gospel stories, Jesus often stayed at their house, a place where he obviously felt comfortable and at home. We don't know why these three lived together or why Mary and Martha did not have husbands. They might have been widowed, but the Bible does not tell us this, and there are no children in their household.

We know only that these two sisters and their brother

shared a home and were close friends of Jesus, and that Jesus was a frequent guest in their home—which brings us to the familiar story of conflict between Martha and Mary. Most women can understand the stress of hosting a dinner for an important person and his friends. In this case, we find Martha busy hosting Jesus and his disciples, while her sister, Mary, oblivious to household chores, was seated at Jesus' feet, listening to his every word. This went on for a while before Martha, exhausted and irritated, finally dared to complain to Jesus about her sister's failure to help her.

> Now as they went on their way, he entered a village; and a woman named Martha received him into her house. And she had a sister called Mary, who sat at the Lord's feet and listened to his teaching. But Martha was distracted with much serving; and she went to him and said, "Lord, do you not care that my sister has left me to serve alone? Tell her then to help me." (Luke 10:38–40)

Especially if you have a sister yourself, you can imagine the scene that might have preceded Martha's complaint to Jesus. She probably started out with good intentions, happy to host Jesus and serve all her guests. As she stressed and slaved, though, perhaps she began to wonder where the heck Mary was. At that time, household chores and meal preparations were entirely the domain of women, and as the two women of the household, both Martha and Mary would have been expected to serve their guests.

SO MANY THINGS TO WORRY ABOUT

Technically Mary *was* shirking household duties when she sat listening at Jesus' feet. Martha might have politely tried to hint to Mary that she could use some help in the kitchen, but so engrossed in all Jesus was teaching her, Mary would have missed the hints. By the time Martha—the older sister, the responsible one—had grown irritated enough to complain to Jesus, there must have been steam coming from her ears. Surely Jesus should come to her rescue!

But Jesus surprised her (and perhaps us, too) with his answer. "Martha, Martha, you are anxious and troubled about many things; one thing is needful. Mary has chosen the good portion, which shall not be taken away from her" (Luke 10:41–42).

Um, what, Jesus? What about the roast? The dishes? The drinks? You mean to say there is something more important going on here?

I once hosted a dinner for my husband's boss and some of his coworkers on a hot summer day. I planned the perfect menu and made up a minute-by-minute schedule to follow so the grilled chicken, rice pilaf, vegetables, and chilled dessert would all come out perfectly. And they did. The food was very good, but by the end of the evening, as our guests were saying good-bye, I realized that I personally couldn't consider my dinner party a success. I had been so rushed and stressed about preparing the food that I had failed to connect with our guests. I might have had a few distracted conversations, but for the most part, I had not enjoyed their company at all, choosing instead to focus on grill temperatures and whipped cream. Just like Martha, I had missed the point.

I have great sympathy for Martha, and I think Jesus did, too. I can almost see the twinkle in his eye as he chided her, "Martha, Martha, you are anxious and troubled about many things."

I love that he said her name twice like that. He knows our lost souls need gentle direction sometimes. Can you imagine him saying your name this way? He knows your name. Imagine the sound of Jesus repeating it to get your attention. He knows you and loves you personally, and he wants your attention, too, just as he wanted Martha's.

At the sound of Jesus' words, Martha's eyes were opened to what was really going on. Jesus was in her living room! And yet she had allowed pride to focus her attention on less important things, even to the point where she accused Jesus himself of not caring about her. Though Luke does not tell us how Martha responded to Jesus in that moment, we can imagine that she was humbly refocused on what was important. Jesus showed her where her faith was lacking, and she allowed it to grow.

We see evidence of her growing faith in future events, especially upon the death of her brother, Lazarus. When this happened, it was Martha who went to Jesus first, to affirm her faith in him: "When Martha heard that Jesus was coming, she went and met him, while Mary sat in the house. Martha said to Jesus, 'Lord, if you had been here, my brother would not have died. And even now I know that whatever you ask from God, God will give you'" (John 11:20–22).

WHAT IS THE BETTER PART?

So what exactly is this "better part," this "one thing" Jesus spoke about? What is the thing that Mary chose and Martha was learning to choose over all other things?

It's a relationship with Jesus. Mary, the sister of great faith, had chosen to focus on Jesus. She sat at his feet and focused her attention only on him, living and breathing every word he spoke.

Have you ever sat at someone's feet? Many of us have as children, perhaps listening to a teacher, parent, or grandparent tell us a story, and that is why Mary's childlike posture in this scene is such a beautiful image of humility and receptivity. You don't sit at someone's feet unless you love him, respect him, and want to be sure not to miss anything he has to say.

WORSHIP IS MORE IMPORTANT THAN WORK

Jesus did not tell Martha that she was doing anything wrong by preparing a meal and working in the kitchen, but by calling Mary's choice the "good portion" he reminds us all that worship is more important than work. Feeding our souls is more important than feeding our bodies.

We all must work, and women who run households know this better than anyone. When this Bible story is read at Mass, my own mother—a wife of forty-eight years and a mom of nine—likes to say that by the time all the talking was done, she's sure Jesus and his disciples were pretty glad *someone* had thought to prepare a meal.

I'm not going to argue with my mom. Practical things are important, and there is always work that must be done, but Jesus does not want us to forget that a relationship with him is *always* the better part. We can be worried and anxious about "many things," but we must make time in our days, and especially in our busy minds, to sit at the feet of Jesus. It is there we find our purpose and our strength.

Mary wasn't doing or saying anything when she chose the good portion. She wasn't accomplishing anything that the world (especially her sister!) would recognize as valuable work, but she had the "one thing" needed. And we can have it, too. We just need to put our "many things" in perspective and focus on our relationship with Jesus. He is eager to help us do this, and just like Mary, when we choose the good portion, it will not be taken from us.

JUST ONE TOUCH

When considering women of great faith in the Bible, we must include the story of the woman who suffered with a hemorrhage. In chapter four we will look at the ways in which her painful suffering affirms the dignity and worth of all women, but for now, let's look beyond her physical condition and consider her spiritual one.

> And there was a woman who had had a flow of blood for twelve years, and who had suffered much under many physicians, and had spent all that she had, and was no better but rather grew worse. She had heard the reports about Jesus, and came up behind him in the crowd and touched his garment. For she said, "If I touch even his garments, I shall be made well." (Mark 5:25–28)

I always marvel at the beautiful simplicity of this woman's approach to Jesus. "If I touch even his garments . . ." Can't you just feel her faith?

For years doctors had failed this poor woman, and money could not buy her a cure—yet she just somehow knew that if she touched the clothing of this Jesus fellow, she would be healed. She needn't bother the man by speaking to him. So great was his power, she believed she could be healed merely by touching his cloak. And that is exactly what happened.

Have you ever been hesitant to pray for something because you didn't want to "bother" God with it? Or have you ever thought, even as you were praying for something good to happen, that there was no way it could ever come to pass?

These are human ways to approach God, and while it might feel like they are reasonably cautious sometimes, when we do these things, we forget who God is. When we are cautious, when we put limits or conditions on our belief, our words and actions demonstrate the weakness of our faith. We forget that God can do anything. How often throughout the Gospel stories do we see Jesus exasperated by people's lack of faith?

"Oh, you of little faith!" we hear him cry out time and again. In this passage, however, when he finds a woman of great faith, he shows us that strong faith will be rewarded: "But the woman, knowing what had been done to her, came in fear and trembling and fell down before him, and told him the whole truth. And he said to her, 'Daughter, your faith has made you well; go in peace, and be healed of your disease'" (Mark 5:33–34).

Imagine the drama of this scene. Because of her faith, this woman, despite her "fear and trembling," had the courage to speak to Jesus and be completely honest. She fell down before him and told him the whole truth. Completely vulnerable and completely trusting, she submitted her entire self to him. And that's exactly what Jesus wanted.

Strength of faith is deeply personal. The woman in this passage demonstrated the kind of devotion, trust, and strong faith Jesus longs to see from each of us. He wishes for each of us to have such confidence in his goodness that we just know he will do good things for us. Jesus, who hung bleeding on a cross and died specifically for the salvation of each of us, longs for each of us to give ourselves over to him completely in return.

Do you hold yourself back and put limits on God's power? Or do you trust in his unlimited power, strength, and goodness? The challenge is to be like Martha, who even in the face of her brother's death told Jesus she knew God could do all things; or like Mary, who was so in love with Jesus that she could see and hear nothing else; or like the woman with a hemorrhage, who knew Jesus would heal her if she just touched his cloak, and so she fell down before him and held nothing back.

OF FAITH AND DOGS

Another woman of great faith in the Bible is the one whom Jesus called a dog. That's right. A dog. Let's take a look.

And behold, a Canaanite woman from that region came

out and cried, "Have mercy on me, O Lord, Son of David; my daughter is severely possessed by a demon." But he did not answer her a word. And his disciples came and begged him, saying, "Send her away, for she is crying after us." He answered, "I was sent only to the lost sheep of the house of Israel." But she came and knelt before him, saying, "Lord, help me." And he answered, "It is not fair to take the children's bread and throw it to the dogs." She said, "Yes, Lord, yet even the dogs eat the crumbs that fall from their master's table." Then Jesus answered her, "O woman, great is your faith! Be it done for you as you desire." And her daughter was healed instantly. (Matthew 15:22–28)

I always follow this conversation with amazement. Can you even imagine? *A dog!* He compared her to a dog, and yet still her faith persisted.

I've heard homilies in which the priest explains that the actual translation of the word used in this Bible story is a cute or affectionate term for *dog*, so that when Jesus said "dog," it was not heard by the woman as offensive in quite the same way it sounds to our ears today. Now, I don't know about you, but though it's not as bad as being called a dog, I actually don't want to be called a puppy or a doggy either.

Either way, the most important part of this passage, and likely the reason Jesus allowed it to continue in such a seemingly harsh manner, is the woman's persistent faith, even in the face of rejection. A Canaanite, the woman in this story was a Gentile, and Jesus was correct in saying that he came first for the Jews. They were his chosen people, and he belonged to them first.

FINDING FAITH THAT PERSISTS

When the woman called out to Jesus, he first ignored her: "He did not answer her a word." She, unfazed by this snub, persisted in her petition.

Do you ever get the sense that God is ignoring your prayers? I certainly have felt that way. At times it can seem as though we are sending our prayers out into a vast and empty space. We don't always experience the consolation of personal conversation and connection with God.

As with the Canaanite woman, however, perhaps Jesus is "ignoring" us for our own good, to test and strengthen our faith. So what do you do when God's answer is not obvious and immediate? Do you persist in prayer, or do you throw in the towel, thinking, "Oh well, I tried. I guess God doesn't care right now"? Sometimes, with his silence, Jesus is refining our prayer. This story shows what can happen when we persist even without hearing a response, as the Canaanite woman did.

JESUS LIKES A STUBBORN FAITH

Even though Jesus ignored her plea, "Lord, help me," the woman persisted. And it was then that Jesus tested her faith even more. This time, whether the official translation is "doggy" or "dog," what came across was a humiliating rebuke.

Does God sometimes give us humiliations to bear? It sure seems that way at times, especially when we cry out to him and our petitions feel unheard or even rebuffed.

Through this series of rejections and humiliations, though, Jesus refined the Canaanite woman's prayer of petition until it achieved the perfection of humility. Instead of recoiling in offense at the mention of the word *dog*, she embraced Jesus' analogy and humbly begged him for the scraps she knew would fall from the master's table.

It is Jesus who gave her the grace, in every step of their conversation, to lose herself in her petition and focus more and more on him alone. He does the same for us in our prayers. Jesus doesn't want us to pray because he needs to hear us tell him how great he is. He is God. He needs nothing. He wants us to pray because *we* need the fruits of our prayer. We need to lose ourselves until we become less focused on ourselves and more focused on Jesus. And when we lose ourselves, we lose the inferior version of ourselves, paving the way for Jesus to reveal our true strength and beauty.

When Jesus praised the Canaanite woman's faith and rewarded her by healing her daughter, it was a great testimony to God's love of persistent prayer. He came for the Jews first, but he responded to even a Gentile's petition because she was confident, persistent, and humble in her request.

IN PERSON
HE WAITS FOR US

Renee was raised Catholic. She made her first Communion and was confirmed along with all the other kids in her parish. She went to Mass every week with her parents and two brothers while growing up. When she got older and could choose for herself, though, she went to church less and less often, and she almost never prayed. By the time she graduated from college, she had walked away from her faith altogether.

"Believing in God felt like something from my childhood," she says. "When I got into the 'real world' with parties and boyfriends and starting my first real job, all those stories about Jesus and the saints felt like fairy tales to me. There wasn't some big dramatic moment where I rejected God, but he just became less real to me."

Renee found a good job working in marketing for a large company and moved to Boston. There she became friends with many young people at her workplace and eventually fell in love with one of her coworkers.

"He was so handsome and smart," she recalls. "I had been in

relationships before, but I never felt this way about a guy. You could not have gotten me to believe anything bad about him." One night, when they were out with mutual friends, the guy she liked finally kissed her, and Renee wound up going home with him and spending the night.

"I was so sure this was it. We were going to be amazing together," she says.

After they hung out a few more times, though, Renee was crushed when her love interest stopped calling and even started avoiding her at work.

"I was so confused," she says. "Because to me, everything about us being together seemed perfect. I couldn't believe he didn't see that."

She moved on from that relationship, but she could not escape the sense of emptiness she felt from the rejection.

"I started to wonder what the point was. Aren't we supposed to fall in love and then live happily ever after? I was missing something—and somehow, I knew it wasn't just that guy I was missing. I needed something else."

Renee found herself lying awake at night, wondering what the purpose of her life was. And that was when, after she'd spent years pushing him aside as a "fairy tale," her heart turned back to God. She tried to remember some of the prayers she had memorized as a little girl.

"I would lie awake at night feeling so alone and just try to say one Hail Mary," she says. "I'm sure I messed up all the words, but I still felt like maybe there was something there."

Renee looked up the old prayers she had once known and began to say them each morning and each night. She looked for a Catholic church and was surprised to find one right in her own neighborhood, within walking distance of her apartment.

"I went there one day after work and just sat inside. Everything was so quiet and familiar; it felt like home. Even the smell of the candle wax made me think of being a little girl. And then I just cried. I probably sat there for an hour, crying like a baby about I don't even know what."

In many ways Renee did go home that day. That first visit to the church was the start of many others, and eventually she started going to Mass again and even made an appointment to go to confession. These days, she attends Mass every week and prays every day. God is real to her again.

"The funny thing about when I thought I left God behind," she says, "is that I never really did. I can see now that he was always right there with me, even when I wasn't paying any attention. He was waiting for me to come back."

SUCH GREAT FAITH

It can be easy to marvel at the strong faith of women in the Bible and feel that they are somehow different from the rest of us. Maybe they got that special "faith gene" at birth, so believing comes easy for them. But we lack that gene. We have doubts, struggles, and weaknesses.

But one look at these real women's lives and we know that is not the case. The examples of Martha and Mary show us how we can vary in personality and temperament, and that these do affect our approach to Jesus, but despite that, every one of us is called to an intimate, soul-feeding relationship with Jesus. Sitting at his feet and listening to his every word will come about differently for each of us, but every one of us was created to be there and to do that. Our hearts, minds, and souls were made for communion and connection with Jesus.

Sometimes, too, we find Jesus in our weakness. Like Renee, we might reject God, or we might find ourselves alone and feeling empty, but that is when God becomes our strength. He meets us in our weakness and lets us know that he is with us. Once we make a first tiny step toward faith, Jesus rushes in to strengthen us.

As Martha stumbled on her way toward Jesus and found her faith eventually strengthened, so, too, can we work with our natural inclinations and learn to find Jesus through them.

Are you "anxious and troubled about many things" (Luke 10:41)? I sure am. Depending on the day of the week, the things worrying me might be car payments, editorial deadlines, bickering children, dinner plans, or the health problems of various family members. We all have our many things, but even as we fret, Jesus waits for us. He smiles patiently as we fuss about anything and everything the way Martha did, and then gently he urges us to focus on the one thing needed.

Jesus wants every part of us. He wants our problems, our worries, our broken bodies, and our broken hearts. He waits for us to silence our preoccupation with pots and pans and instead turn to him with total trust, giving him all that we have and all that we are. He waits for us to fall down before him, as the healed woman with the hemorrhage did.

Even as we go about our busy lives, our hearts and minds are restless until we rest in Jesus. Make the effort now to silence your many things and listen instead to the voice of Jesus within. You may not have the courage yet to reach toward him, but he is speaking to you now. Let's stay there for just a moment, sitting at his feet. Look into his eyes and pray with me:

> *Jesus, I am here. I know you are with me, but still I am small, weak, and distracted. I am worried about many things, but I want to know the one thing that is needed. Help me to know you. I am afraid of changing my life, but I know you can make my faith grow stronger. I want to touch you now and know that you are real. I want to be strengthened. Amen.*

CHAPTER THREE

YOU ARE WHOLE

"Those who are well have no need of a physician,
but those who are sick; I came not to call the
righteous, but sinners."

(MARK 2:17)

I learned a lot about how much Jesus loves us and stays with us from a mother-in-law I never really had.

Dan and I were married in July, and in November of that same year, his mother, Dolores, suffered a debilitating stroke. Though she lived for two more years, we never really got her back. Occasionally, we would see brief flashes of her old personality, but for the most part, she had reverted to a childlike state, often forgetting the names and faces of even those she loved the most.

Dolores was a loving mother who longed for grandchildren and anticipated the future with great joy. Now, though, from one visit to the next, she did not even remember that we were expecting her first grandchild. I remember one visit when she noticed my growing belly and her eyes grew wide.

"Is it . . . Danny's?" she whispered in a panic. *"What are we going to do?"*

I laughed, but then tears stung my eyes. She thought I was the girl her son had dated in high school. A baby would be a scandal.

In the following years, as Dolores' health further deteriorated and she was diagnosed with cancer, we worried about supporting my father-in-law, who cared for her at home, but we also worried about Dolores' spiritual health. She had been raised as a Catholic but had fallen away from the Church as a young adult. She always held on to some parts of her faith, however, and she beamed with pride the day that Dan was confirmed as a Catholic during his college years. We prayed for her health and healing, but in her current state, we weren't sure exactly how to support Dolores spiritually. We should have known that Jesus would take care of that, though.

One day, shortly after Dolores was hospitalized with a serious case of pneumonia, my mother surprised us by letting us know that Dolores had called her. Although my mother and Dolores knew each other, they had never been close friends. There were only a few occasions in her previous life when Dolores would have dialed my mother's phone number, but somehow now, in a hospital room by herself, with even her vision failing, she had recalled the number, dialed it from her bedside phone, and said hello to a woman she had not spoken to in many months.

Believing there must be a reason for the phone call, my mother went to the hospital straightaway. The two exchanged small talk for a few moments before my mother was inspired to ask Dolores if she might like to talk with a priest.

"Oh, yes, please!" came her immediate response.

And my mother knew just the priest to call. Father Dan was a newly ordained priest in our diocese, and he agreed to come visit Dolores the very next day. As soon as Dolores caught sight of Fr. Dan standing in her doorway, wearing his collar, she cried out with surprise and asked, "Are you . . . are you . . . a *Father*?" When he answered yes, Dolores dissolved into tears. For several long minutes, she sobbed uncontrollably.

It was Jesus, her priest, and he had come to see her.

Patiently Fr. Dan sat at her bedside, listening and asking questions. He helped talk Dolores through a general confession, blessed her, anointed her, and left her with a promise of future visits.

We grieved when we lost Dolores a short while later, and Fr. Dan celebrated her funeral Mass, but there was such peace and joy in knowing she had reconciled with God and the Church before leaving us.

When I think of my mother-in-law, alone and trapped in her frail body with a faltering mind, I know the goodness of a God who seeks us. This is the definition of steadfast love. Even if we forget him, even if we are lost and broken, even if we are helpless and others cannot reach us, he comes for us. Dolores knew Jesus when she prayed as a small child, and then she moved on in many ways. But he never left; he sought her out decades later, just when she needed him most.

We cannot run and we cannot hide. Our God is a loving God, a good God, and a personal God who seeks us, finds us, and loves us wherever we are and wherever we go.

During his time on earth, Jesus sought out those who needed him and healed them, both physically and spiritually. Let's take a look at the stories of some of the women he touched, helped, and healed.

BEFORE WE ASK

"I shouldn't have to *ask* my husband to help with the kids at bedtime, should I?" a girlfriend recently complained to me.

Perhaps in an ideal world, husbands would anticipate our every need and rush to our aid, but we all know that sometimes we do need to ask for help. Even the most loving of husbands is not a mind reader, and communication between the sexes is often flawed and complicated.

But has anyone ever anticipated a need of yours and met it before you even thought to ask for help? If so, I'll bet you felt authentically loved and cared for in that moment. We all long for love like that. Having someone else pay attention to the details of our situation and consider our perspective makes us feel uniquely known and loved.

While our human relationships frequently fall short of this

ideal, when it comes to love, Jesus sets an example of perfection. Consider, for example, his encounter with a widow in Nain:

> Soon afterward he went to a city called Nain, and his disciples and a great crowd went with him. As he drew near to the gate of the city, behold, a man who had died was being carried out, the only son of his mother, and she was a widow; and a large crowd from the city was with her.
>
> And when the Lord saw her, he had compassion on her and said to her, "Do not weep." And he came and touched the bier, and the bearers stood still. And he said, "Young man, I say to you, arise." And the dead man sat up, and began to speak. And he gave him to his mother. (Luke 7:11–15)

Imagine the depths of grief this woman suffered as she followed the body of her dead son out of the city. She had already lost her husband, and now her only child had been taken from her as well. This was a devastating loss for her—not only emotionally but socially and economically as well. Without a man to provide for them, women at the time were unable to own property or earn a living for themselves.

Can you picture the bleakness this woman faced as she buried all hope, walking helplessly behind the body of her son? Now imagine the shock of encountering a stranger who commanded her son to return to life—and then watching as her beloved dead son sat up and began talking!

The widow did not know Jesus was there. She did not ask for his help. She might not have even known who Jesus was, but he knew her. He saw her plight, heard her cries, and was filled with compassion. She didn't need to say a word.

Even if you do not know Jesus, you can rest assured that he knows you. He knows everything about you, even things you have never spoken of, and he loves you as you are, with a unique and infinite love.

Jesus saw the widow, who did not see him, and he was deeply moved by his love for her. This is the kind of love Jesus has for each of us. He is filled with pity at the sight of our suffering. He is overcome with compassion for us and longs to end our pain, comfort us in our sorrow, and give us everything we need.

DO NOT WEEP

The simple words Jesus spoke to the widow in this scene are especially moving: "Do not weep." Another person might be tempted to make a grand speech or put on a dramatic show on the momentous occasion of raising someone from the dead. Perhaps there is a deeper lesson we might all learn from this miraculous event, if only a teacher would elucidate it for us. But Luke tells us only three words that Jesus spoke to the grieving woman.

"Do not weep."

We are not all grieving widows, but each of us weeps in her own way. Each of us suffers loss and the pains of imperfection during our time here on earth. It is during our periods of grief and sorrow that Jesus speaks a message of hope and joy to each of us: "Do not weep." Even when we don't know he is with us, Jesus sees our suffering, cares deeply about our well-being, and longs to bring us a message of healing after hurt and life after death.

Are there ways you are "weeping" in your life right now? What is hurting you? Have you suffered emotional wounds from past or current relationships? Are you grieving a loss? Has someone rejected you and made you feel small? Do you struggle with anxiety and depression? Do you have health issues that make you hate your body at times?

Open your hurting heart to Jesus and allow him to see where you are wounded. He alone can touch you, heal you, and bring you new life.

FRUIT OF HIS TOUCH

Simon's mother-in-law was another woman who was helped by Jesus. This was a far less dramatic incident than raising the widow's son from the dead, but significant nonetheless. Mark tells us what happened in just a few quick lines: "Now Simon's mother-in-law lay sick with a fever, and immediately they told him of her. And he came and took her by the hand and lifted her up, and the fever left her; and she served them" (Mark 1:30–31).

This happens at a time in the Gospel story when Jesus' fame had begun to spread. He had difficulty traveling sometimes because of the large numbers of people who sought him out and followed him. Word spread about Jesus' power and the miracles he performed. When we read the Gospel straight through here, the sheer volume of healings taking place is overwhelming. Everywhere Jesus went, the sick and the lame came to him and followed him. Everywhere he went, he reached out, touched people, and healed them.

In the story of Simon's mother-in-law, we find more of the same. Jesus encountered a sick woman, touched her, and bam! She was healed. This quick little story of her healing might easily get lost in the dozens of others, many of which are more climactic, but one thing stands out. In the last line, Mark tells us that "the fever left her; and she served them."

A woman who had been lying sick in bed got up and waited on others. Not only does this detail emphasize the dramatic contrast between Simon's mother-in-law's health before and after Jesus' touch, it tells us something more about Jesus. It tells us that the fruit of his touch is service.

Throughout the Gospels, Jesus calls us to service. He spells out this call clearly in words, but even more so by his own example: ". . . [W]hoever would be great among you must be your servant, and whoever would be first among you must be slave of all. For the Son of man also came not to be served but to serve, and to give his life as a ransom for many" (Mark 10:43–45).

This was the great paradox of Jesus' life. He was a king—God himself!—who came not to be served, but to serve. He came not only to help and to heal, but to give his very life as ransom for those who are subject to him. And he calls us to serve others, too—not because he wishes to humiliate us, but because he knows it is through self-giving love that we will find meaning in our lives. Human beings are built for relationship, and human relationships find meaning through mutual communion and giving ourselves in service to one another.

But how many of us forget this final step in the process of healing? Once we get what we want, once the pain is removed, once we are healed, how many of us take our well-being for granted and forget that we have a call to service?

As I typed the story of my own mother-in-law's healing at the beginning of this chapter, I remembered how dramatically the story affected me at the time, but realized how infrequently I think about it now, years later. I take God's goodness for granted and forget that the fruit of his touch, in our own lives and in the lives of those we care for, is meant to be self-giving love. Jesus' presence in our lives and generous care for our needs should continually inspire us to give more selfless love toward others.

I needed the reminder.

DO NOT FEAR

Remember the woman with the hemorrhage and how her touch interrupted Jesus when he was on a mission to help someone else? Let's take a look now at who that someone else was and what Jesus did for her.

The one in need of healing in this story was the daughter of Jairus, a synagogue official. She was so sick that her family was afraid she would die, and so Jairus came to beg Jesus to help her: "Seeing him, he fell at his feet, and besought him, saying, 'My little daughter is at the point of death. Come and lay your hands on her, so that she may be made well, and live'" (Mark 5:22–23).

Jesus agreed to go to her, but as they traveled, news arrived that it was too late. The daughter had already died. "While he was still speaking, there came from the ruler's house some who said, 'Your daughter is dead. Why trouble the Teacher any further?' But ignoring what they said, Jesus said to the ruler of the synagogue, 'Do not fear, only believe'" (Mark 5:35–36).

Now, if ever you are going to pay close attention to a message, it should probably be when someone tells you someone has died, correct? One would think. But here, once again, Jesus shows us that none of the usual rules apply to him.

Unthinkably, he disregarded the news of the young girl's death and instead told her father to not be afraid and just have faith. He then went to the little girl and, despite the ridicule of those around him, announced that she was not dead at all, but only sleeping.

> And when he had entered, he said to them, "Why do you make a tumult and weep? The child is not dead but sleeping." And they laughed at him. But he put them all outside, and took the child's father and mother and those who were with him, and went in where the child was.

> Taking her by the hand he said to her, "Talitha cumi"; which means, "Little girl, I say to you, arise." And immediately the girl got up and walked; for she was twelve years old. And immediately they were overcome with amazement. (Mark 5:39–42)

First of all, let's just pause for a moment here to bask in the inspiring image of Jesus holding this young girl's hand as she "slept." Think of the love he had for her in that moment. That's the way he looks at us, too. We are his precious daughters; he has that same love for each of us.

In some ways, we, too, are asleep. Even those of us who are lost causes in the eyes of the world, whether because of physical illness or some other problem, weakness, or deficiency, can be revived and made new by the touch of Jesus, but our fear gets in the way.

Why are we so afraid?

The Bible quotes Jesus speaking the words he spoke to

Jairus, "Do not fear," and similar phrases more than one hundred times. His patient repetition must have something to do with our stubborn human hearts; we are slow to trust and quick to panic. But just as he did with the grieving widow, Jesus longs to show us his merciful love. Just as he did with Jairus and his sleeping daughter, he calls on us to get up, reject fear, and follow him.

How will we respond? Will we ever stop sleeping and wake up?

JESUS, THE HERO

One of the most dramatic stories in the Bible is that of the woman who was caught in adultery. The story begins with some petty, jealous scribes and Pharisees who were hoping to trip up Jesus by putting him in an uncomfortable situation.

> Then the scribes and the Pharisees brought a woman who had been caught in adultery and made her stand in the middle. They said to him, "Teacher, this woman was caught in the very act of committing adultery. Now in the law, Moses commanded us to stone such women. So what do you say?" They said this to test him, so that they could have some charge to bring against him. (John 8:3–6)

They hoped to force Jesus to either condemn a woman to death or blatantly defy the law of Moses, neither of which would be a great PR move for a young prophet on the rise. How small-minded and shortsighted they were, though! Jesus was not the success-seeking young hopeful they thought he was, and he did not operate within the confines of their small world with its old rules. They had no idea they were about to experience some public embarrassment of their own.

> Jesus bent down and wrote with his finger on the ground. And as they continued to ask him, he stood up and said to them, "Let him who is without sin among you be the first to throw a stone at her." And once more he bent down and wrote with his finger on the ground. But when they heard it, they went away, one by one, beginning with the eldest, and Jesus was left alone with the woman standing before him. (John 8:6–9)

In this brief story our hearts immediately go out to the woman who is a victim of the scribe and Pharisee bullies. This is surely a woman who has seen her share of mistreatment at the hands of men. We don't know the details of her circumstances, but we do know that she wasn't caught committing adultery by herself. There was a man involved, but he was nowhere to be found, and she had been left to face the consequences of their sin alone.

The Pharisees were simply next in a long line of men

using this woman for their own selfish purposes, but Jesus, the hero of this story, didn't let them get away with it. And he was so cool about it, too. Writing in the sand, waiting for their response. . . . What on earth did he write? Some suggest that he wrote out the sins of those around him, shaming them into dropping their stones and leaving, but the Bible does not tell us what he wrote.

What we do know is that the Pharisees threw this sinful woman at the feet of the wrong guy. If this were a movie or a romance novel, here would be the climactic scene in which we swoon as the hero takes on the bad guys and saves the lady in distress. Here at last, this woman, abused by men and drowning in a sea of sin and shame, meets a man who protects her, defends her, and affirms her dignity.

THE SHAME OF SEXUAL SIN

The fact that this story involves a sexual sin is significant. Sexual sin, as common as it is and has been throughout the ages, carries with it a special burden of shame. Because sex is such a sacred and powerful part of the human experience, when we misuse it, we can feel an especially deep and shameful stigma. Sexual sin leaves us feeling dirty, used, and broken. And yet Jesus did not condemn the woman caught in it. He forgave her: "Jesus looked up and said to her, 'Woman, where are they? Has no one condemned you?' She said, No one, Lord.

And Jesus said, 'Neither do I condemn you; go, and do not sin again'" (John 8:10–11).

What must it have felt like for this woman to find herself flung at the feet of a stranger, her deepest and most shameful secrets laid bare, fearing the very real possibility that she would be stoned to death at any moment? She did not choose to fall down at the feet of Jesus; she was thrown there. But Jesus didn't care how she got there. He defended her, loved her, and forgave her.

We can be afraid to approach God, especially when we are ashamed of things we have done. The example of the woman caught in adultery, however, should give each of us confidence in approaching Jesus. Whatever your sin, whatever the cause of your shame, Jesus will not condemn you. He will love you and forgive you. We must never be afraid to approach Jesus for forgiveness. If we run away and hide out of shame, we will experience only deeper pain and sorrow. Shame keeps us from throwing ourselves at the feet of Jesus, but he alone is the source of grace, healing, and forgiveness.

SIN NO MORE

Sin is real. We see its effects all around us, from the evening news to our dysfunctional families. It's more than just our behavior, too. It's a deep-seated turning away from God and his goodness. Jesus came to establish a new way of being, one steeped in mercy, forgiveness, and love, but he also fully acknowledged the existence and destructive power of sin.

When Jesus told the woman in this story to go and sin no more, he acknowledged the reality of her sin. Though his focus was on mercy and love, he didn't give her a free pass to do as she pleased, nor does he give it to any of us. Sin is real. It destroys us. Sadly, even though we all sin, sometimes we condemn ourselves so harshly that we lose confidence in God's forgiveness. We might refuse to acknowledge our sins and avoid making ourselves vulnerable before him because we consider ourselves unworthy of forgiveness.

But every one of us is a sinner. Each of us truly lies at the feet of Jesus, whether we throw ourselves there willingly or not.

Look up. There, in his loving eyes, you will find mercy, forgiveness, and love.

IN PERSON
HE HEALS OUR HURTS

Kathy was married for three years and pregnant with her second child when she found out about her husband's affair. On a computer they shared, she saw some Facebook messages between him and a high school girlfriend that confirmed something terrible. Her husband, Dave, was spending time with another woman on secret days off from work. He was telling her she looked sexy and that he couldn't wait to be with her.

"I wanted to throw up and cry and punch him in the face all at the same time," Kathy says. "I knew he was stressed at work, and I wondered why he was so angry with me sometimes, but now I knew what was really going on."

Kathy confronted Dave, and he confessed. It was a new relationship, he assured her, and he agreed to end it and get couples counseling. He promised Kathy he loved her and their family more than anything and would do everything he could to make it right.

"I was really hurt and angry, but I also kind of felt bad for him. Is that weird to say? I loved him, and it was sad to me that he could be so weak. He looked pathetic," she says.

She did forgive her husband, and the couple got counseling. By the time their second child was born, they looked like a happy family again, but Kathy still had wounds that hadn't healed.

"I felt so insecure. Dave would be late coming home from work or a pretty woman would walk by, and I would freak out," she says. "I hated feeling like that all the time, but I couldn't help how emotional I felt. Dave was trying so hard that I felt pressured to move on in a way that I wasn't ready to do."

Kathy shared her feelings with a woman she knew from church. Her Catholic faith had always been a part of her life, but now she wondered if perhaps the Church could offer her something more—to help her not only spiritually, but emotionally as well. Her friend encouraged her to come to a women's group that met once a week in the parish hall.

"I went that first night and felt a little out of place," she recalls. "There were a lot of older ladies there, and I had brought the baby with me."

But once the prayer group started, Kathy began to feel more comfortable.

"It was pretty casual," she says. "It wasn't formal like Mass. This was just women sharing some thoughts about a Bible reading, and then praying together."

She went many times before she had the courage to ask the other women to pray for her and her family, but when she did, she experienced a great relief.

"I had such a feeling of love and peace when they prayed for me. I felt like all the tears I had been crying and all those things I was worried about just washed away. I know people always say they will pray for you, and I sometimes used to wonder what that was really worth. But I can tell you, that night their praying was worth a lot to me."

Kathy continued to attend the prayer group, but even more important, she began to value prayer in her own life in a whole new way. Her life is still far from perfect, but her marriage continues to heal, and she knows now that she can turn to God in prayer when she is hurting.

"I used to say prayers, but I never really thought that praying could actually help me in a way that I could know and feel," she says. "Those older ladies taught me something really powerful."

WE ALL NEED HEALING

We might read stories of dramatic healings and miraculous cures and think they don't really apply to us. We aren't dead, we don't have cancer—we don't have even have a hemorrhage. What do we need healing from?

Well, I can't tell you exactly what you need healing from, but I can tell you that we all do need healing. Even if we have no significant health issues, we all suffer the consequences of sin and human weakness, and you don't have to look far to find imperfection in this world. Perhaps you're grieving a loss, perhaps your marriage is struggling, perhaps your children cause you anxiety, or perhaps your work makes you miserable and sad. Perhaps even though everything on the outside looks great, you feel an emptiness inside that you don't know how to fill.

Every one of us is made for a relationship with Jesus. It is through communion with him that we find meaning, purpose, and fulfillment in our lives, and yet so many of us run away. We deny our need, we doubt our worth, we hide in shame, and we fear approaching God.

Think for a moment now about a place in your life where you lack wholeness. Though our details may vary, we are all the same in our need for Jesus. We are the weeping widow, unaware of Jesus' presence; we are the sleeping girl, holding on to Jesus' hand; we are the sinful woman, thrown at Jesus' feet. As we read the Gospel stories and imagine the lives of these women long ago, Jesus speaks life-giving, soul-feeding words in the depths of our hearts.

His words are never complicated. When we are filled with grief and sorrow, he says, "Do not weep." When we are gripped with anxiety, he reminds us, "Do not fear." When we doubt the goodness of God, he says, "Have faith." When we fall down at his feet, "Arise," he tells us, "and sin no more."

When you find yourself flung helplessly at Jesus' feet, will you take the hand he reaches toward you? Will you admit your need for wholeness—will you make yourself vulnerable in his loving presence, and let him touch and heal you?

No matter what kind of healing you need right now, or how you are hurting, Jesus wants to help you. Quiet your mind for just a moment now and pray these words with me:

Jesus, I am hurting. Life has 'flung me at your feet' and I feel helpless. I sometimes hide the ways in which I am hurt inside, but I know you already see me. I need your help and healing, but I don't know how to ask. You see my wounds and you alone can heal me. Touch me now. I want to be healed. I want to be made new. Amen.

CHAPTER FOUR

YOU ARE WORTHY

"I am the good shepherd; I know my own and my
own know me, as the Father knows me and I know the
Father; and I lay down my life for the sheep."

(JOHN 10:14–15)

I used to write articles occasionally for a popular political web-site. When some readers there disagreed with my opinions, their comments were often less an argument against my opinions and more a commentary on the fact that I was female.

"You're ugly," commenters who had never laid eyes on me would let me know, or "You're fat."

Juvenile, for sure, but also sexist. Whether readers agreed with them or not, the men who wrote in that space rarely received comments about their physical appearance. But a woman who dared to voice her opinion was pronounced fat and ugly and therefore useless to the male commenters, and was dismissed out of hand.

No woman is immune. Even those of us who live in lib-erated Western cultures will sometimes find ourselves star-ing into the ugly face of sexism. It might come in the form of those who belittle our opinions or dismiss our intelligence by sexualizing us and calling us demeaning names. It might come in the form of men who see our bodies as sexual objects to be used for their pleasure through pornography, prostitution, or abusive relationships. It might even come in the form of a popular culture that, from the time we are little girls, subtly tells us over and over again that only our looks matter, that we can never be thin enough or pretty enough or sexy enough.

The kind of sexism we face in an "enlightened" culture such as ours can be deeply wounding, but can you imagine living in a culture where men—even your own husband—are forbidden to speak to you in public simply because you are a woman? Can you fathom your rage against injustice in a world where women are seen not only as second-class citizens or the property of men but also as sources of evil and uncleanliness to be shunned and shamed as a result of their natural bodily functions? Welcome to the world of women during the time when Jesus walked the earth.

JESUS AFFIRMS ALL WOMEN

In Jesus' time, a rabbi would have considered it beneath his dignity, if not scandalous, to address a woman, especially in public. Men were permitted to divorce their wives for any reason and leave them with no means of support, but women were not permitted to divorce their husbands. Women had no recourse in a court of law.

Religious sayings of the time actually revealed a deep-seated hatred of women: "Even the most virtuous of women is a witch" and "It is well for those whose children are male, but ill for those whose children are female."[1]

What's more, Jewish women were considered unclean during times of menstruation. They were not to be touched; any clothing, object, or person who came in contact with a menstruating woman was considered impure by association.

While these are disturbingly antifemale laws, customs, and traditions, it is a great balm to our feminine souls when we read in the Bible just how little Jesus cared about breaking religious laws and social customs that oppressed women. Instead, in a refreshingly matter-of-fact manner, he treated women as equal to men in all things. He talked openly with the women he met, taught them, affirmed their dignity, asked them questions, and never avoided their company or their touch.

We have already noted the story of the Samaritan woman at the well and the social barriers Jesus broke in speaking with her. One of the greatest of these barriers, however, was simply the fact that she was a woman. Jesus shocked her first

---

1 Leonard J. Swidler, *Yeshua: A Model for Moderns* (Kansas City, Mo.: Sheed & Ward, 1988), p. 68.

when he addressed her directly and asked for a drink of water, but he also amazed his own disciples, who discovered the two speaking together upon their return: "Just then his disciples came. They marveled that he was talking with a woman . . ." (John 4:27).

And not only did Jesus speak to a woman, but he went on to have a deep and revealing theological conversation with her. In that moment, without saying a word, he conveyed a clear message to the woman at the well—and indeed to all women—about her equality to men in personal dignity and worth. He did not make a grand speech about equality between the sexes, he did not boldly proclaim the equality of every woman to every man, and he did not verbally address the idea that women should be given equal treatment under the law and equal status to men in society. He simply spoke to a woman, spent time with her, and treated her with respect and dignity. These countercultural actions spoke volumes.

The way Jesus defied cultural definitions and the limitations placed upon women would have been anything but matter-of-fact for the people of that time. Time and again, he taught us with the power of his bold example. He spoke to the woman at the well as he would have spoken to a man, and as a result, his entire conversation with her became a remarkable rejection of sexual inequality—a message that is still relevant to women today.

TOUCHED BY GOD

Another striking example of how Jesus treated women with countercultural dignity and respect is the story of the woman whom he healed on the Sabbath.

> And there was a woman who had had a spirit of infirmity for eighteen years; she was bent over and could not fully straighten herself. And when Jesus saw her, he called her and said to her, "Woman, you are freed from your infirmity." And he laid his hands upon her, and immediately she was made straight, and she praised God. (Luke 13:11–13)

When I read this passage, I am most moved by the demonstration of the power of Jesus' physical touch. Have you ever been deeply impacted by the power of someone's physical touch? I once went to confession with a priest I did not know very well and was surprised when he placed his hands on my head as he spoke the words of absolution. Beyond the unexpected gesture, I was surprised by the powerful sensation of healing present in the sacrament that I received through the hands of the priest. It brought tears to my eyes.

How have you experienced the healing and affirming power of human touch? Perhaps the deep significance of a hand placed on a shoulder, or an embrace during a time of difficult forgiveness or deep sorrow? Let's consider for a moment how the crippled woman in this story might have felt upon receiving the touch of Jesus' healing hands.

For eighteen years, this woman had suffered from a crippling infirmity caused by an evil spirit. For eighteen years, she was shunned by her own people because of her ailment. For eighteen years, she had been unable even to stand up. Physical and spiritual suffering were all she had known, and then there she was, minding her own business in the synagogue, when a strange man called out to her. He touched her. He laid his hands on her—a person others avoided, not speaking to her or touching her because she was female and crippled. Fearlessly Jesus called out to her and laid his hands on her. And there, in that moment, she was made new.

In speaking to, touching, and healing her, Jesus affirmed the dignity and worth of this crippled woman whom others had avoided and ignored. Immediately she was full of gratitude to God, but others were less impressed: "But the ruler of the synagogue, indignant because Jesus had healed on the sabbath, said to the people, "There are six days on which work ought to be done; come on those days and be healed, and not on the sabbath day'" (Luke 13:14).

Jesus had already affirmed the dignity and worth of this woman through his actions, but next he did so with his words as well.

Then the Lord answered him, "You hypocrites! Does not each of you on the sabbath untie his ox or his ass from the manger, and lead it away to water it? And ought not this woman, a daughter of Abraham whom Satan bound for eighteen years, be loosed from this bond on the sabbath day?" (Luke 13:15–16)

Imagine the healing power of hearing these words after having felt worthless and useless for eighteen years! After long years of illness and mistreatment that made her feel subhuman, finally someone recognized this woman's suffering with sympathy and love. After years of being shunned and shamed, imagine how she must have felt to be defended as a "daughter of Abraham"—a beloved child of God.

Just as Jesus touched, healed, and affirmed the crippled woman in the synagogue that day, he touches, heals, and affirms all women. Whether we suffer physical ailments or spiritual ones, whether we are crippled by our own sinfulness or by the sinfulness of others, Jesus recognizes our dignity and worth. He longs to touch each of us and make us new.

Do we hear him? Will we let him?

REACHING OUT TO JESUS

Remember when Jesus healed the woman with a hemorrhage? We focused on the strength of her faith in chapter two, but now let's consider a different and especially striking part of her story: the fact that she suffered from abnormal feminine bleeding, a bleeding that went on, nonstop, for twelve years.

Even in today's modern world, any woman can understand the agony of such an ailment. Can you imagine bleeding for years? The physical toll this must have taken on her would be bad enough, but in Jesus' time, her condition would have had devastating social consequences as well.

In first-century Palestine, menstruating women were separated from the rest of society. Their own husbands could not sleep with them. Women who were bleeding were considered unclean and therefore were not to touch or be touched by others, even their own families. In everyday living, they had to be careful not to contaminate any seating surfaces, objects, food, or clothing with their menstrual flow, lest they make others "unclean" by association. Consider the burden of this obligation in the days before Tampax!

Now, I don't want to impose modern-day values on ancient times. Some of us might even think it would be pretty nice to leave our families behind for an all-girl mini-vacation when we have our periods, and I can relate to that. Some theories further suggest that the cyclic separation of men and women was meant as a means to boost fertility, as it served to ensure that married couples would be reunited and have sexual relations during the part of the woman's cycle when she was most likely to conceive a child.

This is all well and good, but still it's hard to ignore the basic injustice of this practice. It's hard to escape the fact that in this patriarchal society, women and young girls were told there was something wrong with them, that they were unclean and untouchable because of the biological consequences of being female. I can't think of a more sexist attitude than that.

But the good news is that Jesus rejected this inhumane, sexist way of thinking. When the woman who was bleeding touched his cloak, he responded immediately.

> She said, "If I touch even his garments, I shall be made well." And immediately the hemorrhage ceased; and she felt in her body that she was healed of her disease. And Jesus, perceiving in himself that power had gone forth from him, immediately turned about in the crowd, and said, "Who touched my garments?" (Mark 5:28–30)

He was not outraged or disgusted by the touch of a bleeding woman. He did not stop to engage in a ritual cleansing to rid himself of contamination, as the laws at the time would have required. He knew that the woman's touch had not, in fact, made him unclean, and instead of disgust or outrage, he felt only compassion. He saw only the great faith of a suffering woman in need of his help. "He said to her, 'Daughter, your faith has made you well; go in peace, and be healed of your disease'" (Mark 5:34).

In this story, Jesus could have healed a woman with a broken arm or a stomach condition. He could have healed a man or a child with any kind of ailment, but this time he did not. This time he chose to heal a woman with a womanly condition, and there is great significance to the intimate, feminine details of this healing.

The prevailing culture in Jesus' time got women wrong, and Jesus used this healing to defy its wrongness. By rejecting cultural definitions and impositions on women, Jesus sent a message of affirmation and acceptance of the goodness, dignity, and worth of every woman.

Jesus' actions tell us that being born a woman is not a bad or unclean thing, and that a feminine need is every bit as important as the request of the important man he was responding to at the time. Jairus, a prominent official, had asked him to save his daughter who was dying. His need was urgent. Because of the touch of a single woman, though, Jesus paused and responded to her particular need. With these actions, he tells us that the physical need of an anonymous, faith-filled woman in the crowd is every bit as pressing as the request of an important male dignitary.

TODAY'S WOMEN, TOO

Clearly Jesus did not consider himself bound by cultural norms and expectations, especially those that were misguided and wrong. He has never been politically correct. When it comes to social attitudes toward women, he is unafraid to defy today's culture, too, and certainly there are ways in which the modern world gets women wrong.

In the modern, Western world, we may not have laws that separate and punish women simply for being women, but there are parts of our culture that reject authentic femininity. The things that make us different from men are some of our greatest strengths; they are the means by which we build relationships and find meaning in our lives. In today's world, as throughout all of history, the uniquely feminine gifts of women unfailingly bless our families, our communities, and our world at large.

Consider, however, the world's attitude toward the uniquely feminine gifts of loving and nurturing others, whether it be through biological motherhood, spiritual motherhood, community relationships, caring for the poor, caring for the elderly, or a religious vocation. Are these kinds of womanly, self-giving love celebrated in our culture, or are they seen as less important than career or business goals?

There may be ways that we as a society give lip service to the value of women who act as caregivers, but do we put our money where our mouths are? Are our economic systems and corporate cultures set up to affirm women who choose to become mothers, nurturers, and caregivers? Are uniquely feminine gifts such as gentleness, compassion, sensitivity, nurturing love, and generosity seen as strengths, or are they seen as weaknesses and embarrassments in our modern world?

Personally, I have experienced enough of both the competitive corporate world and the largely unseen world of at-home parenting to know that in the pursuit of liberation and a cultural definition of success, there are many ways in which our culture encourages modern women to squelch their natural feminine inclinations, hide the very gifts that make them uniquely strong, and seek to become less female and more male in their approach to the world.

We may no longer have menstrual laws and regulations to shun and separate us, but too often our culture rejects the gift of womanhood, looks down on sensitivity, and affirms male definitions of success, often at the expense of what women long for and sense in their hearts they were made for.

But Jesus does not reject who we are. In times both ancient and modern, he affirms every woman's dignity as a unique human being who is worthy of love and infinitely valuable. He embraces those things that make us different from men, and he frees us to reject cultural definitions of who we are and what it means to be a woman. Jesus' words and actions encourage us to accept our natural gifts, celebrate the uniqueness of our femininity, and love others in ways that help us find true happiness and satisfaction in our daily lives.

IN PERSON
FINDING WHOLENESS IN JESUS

For many years, pain was all that Peggy knew. She did not

know the meaning of human dignity, and she surely did not know the depths of Jesus' love. As a child, Peggy suffered horrific physical, emotional, and sexual abuse at the hands of her biological father, in the foster care system, and eventually in the custody of a "Christian" adoptive family. The suffering she endured as a child left scars on her body, but even more so, in her heart.

"I didn't know anything but pain and people who would abandon me. I didn't trust anyone, and from early on, I learned to rely on myself for things," she says.

In the midst of her tumultuous childhood, Peggy first learned about Jesus during a brief time spent in the custody of a loving grandmother in Kansas. Her grandmother encouraged her to accept Jesus as her Savior, and she did.

"She was one person who showed me just a little bit of kindness. The things she told me seemed almost too wonderful to believe. That Jesus could love me? That I was made for something good? I wanted to believe that so much."

Peggy had a gift for taking care of animals, and it was through her interactions with them over the years that she came to understand her longing for the healing touch of Jesus.

"I could look into an animal's eyes and see what it needed. I could get it to trust me because it sensed I wanted to help it," she says. "I loved animals of all kinds, and they loved me. We understood each other."

When at last Peggy became an independent adult and was able to separate herself, at least in part, from her abusive past, she met a wonderful man, Jay, and the two were married. Her new husband was Catholic, and eventually Peggy joined the Catholic Church as well. Because Jay was thought to be infertile due to a childhood case of mumps, though, Peggy knew that one of her greatest longings—to have biological children of her own—was not to be met in her marriage.

"But I knew we could someday adopt a little girl, and that was something I dared to pray for," she says.

The couple made a trip to the Basilica of Our Lady of Guadalupe, in Mexico, and it was there that Peggy asked Jesus, through Mary, to send them a daughter to love. Peggy's prayer was answered in a most unexpected way several years later. She was surprised to find she was pregnant, and she miraculously give birth to a baby girl, Naomi. The couple also eventually adopted a son, and Peggy was overwhelmed by God's mercies as she experienced them through being a mother.

She never forgot her painful past, though, and she felt called to relieve the sufferings of others. She and her husband became foster parents, and over the years they have fostered, loved, and helped to heal the wounds of hundreds of foster children.

"I love every one of them," Peggy says. And she makes sure they know Jesus loves them, too.

"When our foster kids are small, I never tell them to believe in the Tooth Fairy or Santa Claus or anything like that," she says. "I hoped in those things as a child and was always disappointed. But Jesus is real. When you look into the eyes of a frightened child, and they need you, that's where Jesus is. He is human, and he is real."

Despite an unspeakably horrific childhood, Peggy has no doubt about the strength of Jesus' love and affirmation of the person she is today.

"Sometimes people say their faith is like concrete, but my faith is not concrete. Have you seen concrete? It has holes in it! My faith is in the blood of Jesus. There are no cracks in there."

WHERE DO WE SEEK OUR WORTH?

Just like the woman at the well, the woman cured on the Sabbath, and the woman healed of a hemorrhage, Peggy's life-changing encounter with Jesus defied what others had told her about her own dignity and worth. Even in times of terrible suffering, sorrow, and abuse, Jesus' steadfast presence and unfailing love remain unchanged. Time and again, Jesus breaks through cultural and social barriers in his affirmation of women, our unique gifts, and our equal dignity as human beings.

It is perhaps an inevitable consequence of original sin that there will always exist some measure of discrimination against women in this world. Even in cultures where women enjoy the same social privileges as men, our unique feminine gifts and strengths are not always encouraged and appreciated in the way they should be. This rejection strikes at the very heart of what makes women truly happy.

So many of us are not happy. We are torn. Even if we seem to have achieved all kinds of "success," we can feel dissatisfied, and we aren't sure why. I met a new mother at a conference not too long ago. She had three children who were still very small, and yet still she wanted more from life.

"I went to college and have always been very successful in my work," she told me. "I just can't imagine that this is all I am meant to do right now," she said, gesturing at her overloaded stroller.

One thing I always try to emphasize to women who struggle with the concept of being "just a mom," even for a limited time, is that it's OK to struggle, but it's important to know which voices we are listening to, particularly when it comes to our identity as women.

So much of the anxiety I suffered as a young mother could have been avoided if I had listened to the voice of Jesus instead of the noisy voices and values of the world. During those days, as I struggled with my new role as a mother, I needed to hear Jesus tell me that what I was doing and the sacrifices I was making had tremendous value and worth, which was something I knew deep in my heart. Instead, I sometimes gave in to the temptation to apply worldly values to my circumstances, and then, not surprisingly, I would come up short, feeling depleted and unappreciative.

The world was telling me I was not enough, but that is

something Jesus never tells us. He whispers that we are made by God, and that we are good. Our encounters with Jesus might be life changing, but they do not change who we are and the women God made us to be; rather, encountering Jesus shifts our perspective and changes how we view ourselves.

The world might tell you something about your worth. It might tell you that without a "thigh gap" and pouty lips you can never be truly beautiful. It might tell you that you are only as valuable as the paycheck you earn. It might tell you that sex is the only thing you have to offer a man. It might tell you that making sacrifices and giving generously to care for others is foolish nonsense and a waste of your time. It might tell you that wealth and all it can buy are what you should be working for.

The world lies, but Jesus speaks the truth.

Jesus longs to reach you personally with the countercultural message that you are valuable. You are beautiful. You have dignity and worth, not because of anything you have done or anything you have earned, but simply because you are a daughter of God. You are made in his image, and he knows you and loves you precisely as you are: physically, emotionally, and spiritually.

As modern women, do we dare to reject worldly ideas about our value and instead turn our hearts to the voice of Jesus within us? When we seek affirmation and love, do we remember to turn to Jesus, the only one who can give us these things without strings attached?

Through the ages and today, Jesus speaks to us. Only in him can we find affirmation of our true identity as women. Only in him will we find the courage to reject the world's lies about womanhood. Let us open up our hearts now, and allow him to make us new.

Jesus, you teach us that God made women beautiful and good. Help me to see the particular ways that I am beautiful and good and to know that my goodness can be a gift to others. I want to reject the false things other people might tell me about my worth, but it is hard sometimes. Their voices are so strong. Help me to hear your voice instead. Remind me that you love me and that I am precious in your eyes. I want to be affirmed. Amen.

CHAPTER FIVE

YOU ARE HEARD

"Ask, and it will be given you; seek, and
you will find; knock, and it will be opened to you."

(MATTHEW 7:7)

On birthdays in our house, we have a tradition in which family members compete to be the first to say "Happy birthday" to the birthday boy or girl. I have sneaked into a sleeping child's bedroom on some birthdays only to find two or three others already there, waiting to be the first to shout "Happy birthday!" at the stroke of midnight.

It's a silly game, but the feeling behind it is real. There is something special about being the first to bear joyful witness to a happy occasion, and there is no happier occasion than the coming of Jesus. Time and again in the stories of the Bible, we see that it is women who occupy the privileged place of being first to see and know Jesus. From the time Jesus was growing in Mary's womb, to his infancy, to the terrible moments when he suffered a horrific death, to his triumphant resurrection from the dead, Jesus allowed women to be the first to see these events and tell the world about them.

We can know that Jesus respects the voices of women and wants each of us to be heard, because the Bible shows us that he gave women's perspectives and female voices a place of respect and precedence throughout the important stories of his lifetime.

Let's explore the tales of some of these women to see what we can learn from their experiences with Jesus. I think we should begin with a pregnant old lady. Yes, you read that right. One of the first people to know Jesus was an elderly woman who became pregnant. All things are possible with God!

A WOMAN'S VOICE COMES FIRST

Gray-haired, wrinkled, and . . . pregnant? Meet Elizabeth, one character in the Bible who was certain that God has a sense of humor. More important, however, Elizabeth was the first person to recognize who Jesus was and tell the world about it. She, a woman with no political power and little social status, was the first to speak the Good News of Jesus coming to give us forgiveness and new life.

When an angel visited Elizabeth's husband, Zechariah, and told him that after a lifetime of heartache and longing, his elderly, infertile wife at last would conceive and bear a son, Zechariah was incredulous. No, worse than that. He was fearful of the angel and he doubted that the message could be true. For his sin of doubting the power of God, he was rendered mute for the duration of his wife's pregnancy.

For her part, Elizabeth did not doubt, and she, who the Bible tells us was "advanced in years," was most definitely pregnant. An unusual medical case, to be sure, but as the months passed, Elizabeth, who was once barren, grew large with child. The angel Gabriel shared this astonishing piece of news with Mary in Nazareth when he announced that Mary was to be the mother of Jesus: "'And behold, your kinswoman Elizabeth in her old age has also conceived a son; and this is the sixth month with her who was called barren. For with God nothing will be impossible'" (Luke 1:36–37).

Upon hearing this news, Mary went "with haste" to her cousin Elizabeth, in order to be of help to her during the final months of her pregnancy. And it is there, in Judah, where the two women meet, that we find the first account of Jesus' encounter with a human being other than Mary. Unborn baby Jesus, safely hidden away in his mother's womb, may not have said or done anything notable upon meeting Elizabeth, but Elizabeth responded dramatically to his presence.

"Blessed are you among women, and blessed is the fruit of your womb! And why is this granted me, that the mother of my Lord should come to me? For behold, when the voice of your greeting came to my ears, the babe in my womb leaped for joy." (Luke 1:42–44)

No one had told Elizabeth about Mary's pregnancy, and certainly no one had told her that Mary was pregnant with the Son of God. When she heard Mary's greeting, though, she simply knew these things to be true, and she, along with the baby growing inside her, rejoiced at the greatness of God.

Elizabeth was pregnant with the future John the Baptist, a son she was told would be a great prophet, but it was she herself who became the first to speak about Jesus. She was the very first human being to recognize Jesus for who he was—God and our Savior—and she believed in him even without seeing him. Elizabeth's immediate reaction to the presence of Jesus was a joyful exclamation and praise. So great was her faith that she instantly recognized the significance of Mary ("blessed are you among women") and Jesus ("and blessed is the fruit of your womb"). So momentous were Elizabeth's words of joy and praise that the Church has preserved them for all time in the words of the Hail Mary.

Jesus could have revealed himself to an "important" man or a spiritual leader of the time, but he did not. Silent and unborn, he chose Elizabeth, an old woman, a nobody in the eyes of society, to reveal himself to in this special way.

Are you beginning to see that Jesus' ways are not our ways? He reveals himself to each of us in a deeply personal way. He might not come to us physically through our relatives' pregnant bellies, but he still does come, often hidden in our human relationships and everyday circumstances. The challenge before us is to be attentive to his presence, as Elizabeth was, and when we do find him, to proclaim his goodness with joy.

MEET ANNA

Do you know Anna? Perhaps not. She's one of those characters in the Bible who blend in a bit with the background. You can miss her altogether if you're not paying close attention.

Blending in was something that Anna did well, and yet she, too, was among the first to know and love Jesus. After losing her husband early in life, instead of remarrying to secure her future, Anna decided to spend her remaining years in prayer at the temple, praying for and waiting for the Messiah. For decades, she was always there. Always praying. Always waiting. It's easy to miss seeing someone like that.

But God noticed Anna. He rewarded her faithfulness in a special way.

And there was a prophetess, Anna, the daughter of Phanu-el, of the tribe of Asher; she was of a great age, having lived with her husband seven years from her virginity, and as a widow till she was eighty-four. She did not depart from the temple, worshiping with fasting and prayer night and day. And coming up at that very hour she gave thanks to God, and spoke of him to all who were looking for the redemption of Jerusalem. (Luke 2:36–38)

Anna came forward at the very time Simeon was announcing who Jesus was. She could have been occupied somewhere else with her prayers in the temple that day, but God planned that his faithful servant Anna would be present at Jesus' presentation, would hear the blessing of Simeon, understand its meaning, and see Jesus, the one she longed for, with her own eyes.

We might like for the story to get emotional and dramatic here. Perhaps Anna should have fallen to her knees as she clutched the infant Jesus to her chest, but the scene that the Bible describes is much more subdued. Anna "gave thanks to God and spoke of [the child] to all."

As one of the first human beings to recognize who Jesus was, she responded to his presence with thanksgiving and by sharing the Good News with others. Simeon gave an eloquent speech, but Anna, who knew the gift God had given her, simply went about the business of sharing about Jesus with all who could hear. Jesus, a tiny baby, said and did nothing during his visit to the temple; he was there only to be seen and to be loved. And yet he rewarded Anna's loyalty, fasting, and prayers with the special privilege of being among the first to see him and recognize him for who he was.

LOVING BABY JESUS

It seems fitting to me that Jesus came to us as a tiny baby, passive and helpless. We might fear a man or keep our distance from him, especially a strange man, but no one—especially not a woman—fears a baby. Whether we physically bear children or not, women are wired for motherhood, both physically and spiritually. Though not every woman melts at the sight of a sweet baby, many of us do, and every woman is gifted with a special feminine capacity for generosity and nurturing love. This capacity is perfected in caring for those who need our help, be they husbands, infants, teenagers, elderly neighbors, coworkers, or the poor in our communities.

Any woman who is a mother knows the all-encompassing urge to care for her child, even at great cost to herself sometimes. Human relationships mirror divine ones. The bond that a mother naturally forms with her infant child as she feeds him, clothes him, carries him, and sleeps with him is a beautiful reflection of the kind of intimate connection Jesus wants to have with each of us. An infant's helplessness inspires an intimate and intense bond between mother and child. By coming to Anna as a tiny infant, Jesus initiated the intense and loving communion he wants to have with each of us. He wants to give us his whole self, completely and without hesitation, and he invites us to return that love with the gift of ourselves to him.

The beautiful bond Jesus seeks to create with each of us

begins with his infancy. Anna saw him and knew this. Baby Jesus, swaddled in blankets, gazes into our eyes, helpless and needy. He offers his presence to us quietly, without making demands. He seeks only to be loved and to love in return. How will we respond?

MARY MAGDALENE

In movies or books Mary Magdalene is often portrayed as a witch, a priestess, a goddess, or even Jesus' wife. It can be difficult to separate fact from fiction when it comes to this woman.

Perhaps she attracts so much attention from Hollywood because she is an unusually strong female figure in the Bible, one who is mentioned by name many times. Some believe that Mary Magdalene was the woman caught in adultery (see John 8:1) or the sinful woman who anointed Jesus with expensive perfume and cried at his feet (see Luke 7:37–39), but there is no conclusive evidence that she is either of these women.

In fact, since the Bible refers to Mary Magdalene by name numerous times, it seems implausible that these particularly dramatic stories would be told about her anonymously. One thing we do know for certain about her past is that Jesus saved her from a demonic possession. We first meet her in a list of women following Jesus:

And the twelve were with him, and also some women

who had been healed of evil spirits and infirmities: Mary, called Magdalene, from whom seven demons had gone out, and Jo-anna, the wife of Chuza, Herod's steward, and Susanna, and many others, who provided for them out of their means. (Luke 8:1–3)

Imagine the helplessness of being controlled by evil spirits. Imagine the suffering of being possessed by seven demons. Imagine the faith of someone who suffered for years in this condition and then had a life-changing encounter with Jesus himself. That someone is Mary Magdalene.

Out of gratitude and love for Jesus, Mary Magdalene accompanied him, even to a brutal death on the cross. As we read the details of Jesus' life and passion, over and over again the Bible tells us that Mary Magdalene was there, watching and introducing others to him.

GIVING VOICE TO SUFFERING

When the hour of Jesus' passion and death came, we know that women, including Mary Magdalene, were by his side: "But standing by the cross of Jesus were his mother, and his mother's sister, Mary the wife of Clopas, and Mary Magdalene" (John 19:25).

Peter, who so loved Jesus and had professed his loyalty to him just hours before, was nowhere to be found. Mary Magdalene and the other women were there, ministering to him in his suffering. Think of the terrible violence these women must have witnessed, and yet, in their love, they could not bear to turn away from Jesus.

Even today, women play a special role in seeing and giving voice to suffering. Often it is women who speak up for the rights of the poor, the disabled, the unborn, and others who cannot speak for themselves. On battlefields, in hospitals, and in everyday life, women bring dignity to those who suffer.

Jesus allowed this special feminine gift to be highlighted through the loyalty and devotion of Mary Magdalene and other women at the time of his crucifixion. Their steadfast presence in the face of horrific violence speaks to us still. It tells us that this is what real faith looks like. Faith is not some legalistic practice of religion; it is love that remains unchanged, that withstands sacrifice and great suffering. This kind of love is real. It lives, breathes, cries out, and bleeds.

Do you want that kind of love? I do. I want to give it, and I want to receive it.

In her loyalty to Jesus, Mary Magdalene followed him even after his death, secretly watching where he was buried, so she could return later, tend to his body, and give him a proper burial. For this small act of kindness, she was richly rewarded.

SPEAKING THE GOOD NEWS

Because of her faithfulness to Jesus at the time of his death, Mary Magdalene held the special privilege of being the first person to whom he revealed himself after rising from the dead. After coming to the tomb to tend to Jesus' body and finding the tomb empty, Mary feared that someone had taken his body.

No one could have been more certain that Jesus was dead than Mary Magdalene. She saw, up close and in gory detail, the beating, the scourging, the nailing to the cross, and that terrible moment when Jesus breathed his last and gave up his spirit, hanging on the cross. She saw his lifeless body removed from the cross, wrapped hastily in burial cloths, and placed in a tomb. She was certain that Jesus was dead and only concerned herself with caring for his body, but he surprised her with good news instead.

> . . . [S]he turned round and saw Jesus standing, but she did not know that it was Jesus. Jesus said to her, "Woman, why are you weeping? Whom do you seek?" Supposing him to be the gardener, she said to him, "Sir, if you have carried him away, tell me where you have laid him, and I will take him away." Jesus said to her, "Mary." She turned and said to him in Hebrew, "Rabboni!" (which means Teacher). (John 20:14–16)

I don't know about you, but Mary Magdalene quickly becomes my favorite in this passage because she thought Jesus was the gardener. That is precisely the sort of embarrassing mistake I can see myself making. Jesus chooses you—yes, you!—to be the first person to see him after his resurrection, and you think he is the gardener.

Oh, Mary. We love you.

When our vision is blurred by tears, we cannot always see things as they are. When we are suffering and despairing, it is tempting at times to feel utterly alone, but the truth is that we are never alone. Jesus is always with us, and he's present to us in a special way when we suffer. Mary Magdalene demonstrated this in that joyful Easter moment when her tears turned to joy.

Even more revealing of Mary Magdalene's great love for Jesus is the passage that comes next:

> Jesus said to her, "Do not hold me, for I have not yet ascended to the Father; but go to my brethren and say to them, I am ascending to my Father and your Father, to my God and your God." Mary Magdalene went and said to the disciples, "I have seen the Lord"; and she told them that he had said these things to her. (John 20:17–18)

"Do not hold me," Jesus told her. He did not say this in an unkind way, but it is meaningful because throughout the Bible Jesus repeatedly called others to come closer to him, beckoned them to follow him, and encouraged them to hold on to him. But Mary Magdalene loved Jesus so much and was so deeply devoted to him that she needed a different kind of instruction. She clung to him so tightly that he had to tell her to release her grip and go share the good news of his triumphant resurrection with all who would hear. And that is just what she did.

More often than not, we women are the "feelers" of our communities and families. We have a special gift for seeing and caring for those who suffer. We sometimes also have the privilege of speaking out for those who cannot speak for themselves. Jesus knows this, and he calls us to draw closer to him through the poor and the suffering, and even through our own pain and loss. He turns our tears to joy, and then he urges us to share the Good News of his triumph over death.

IN PERSON
STANDING UP AND SPEAKING OUT

When Dena's teenage daughter, Kylie, called to say she was staying after school to talk with a friend about some personal problems, Dena didn't think much of it. Kylie was a caring girl, and her friends often relied on her for sound advice and a sympathetic ear.

When she picked her daughter up a few hours later and saw that her face was streaked with tears, she became alarmed.

But Kylie told her it was nothing, just some "stupid boy problems" her friend Alex was having.

"Something about the way she clammed up worried me," Dena says. "I prayed about it that night, and somehow felt that I shouldn't just let it go. The next day, I pushed Kylie to tell me what was really going on."

Kylie resisted, saying she had promised Alex she wouldn't tell, but she eventually relented. It turned out that a boy Alex had broken up with had some pictures of her on his phone—embarrassing pictures she regretted allowing him to take—and he was now threatening to send them to the entire school if she didn't agree to go out with him again.

"I was shocked," Dena says. "I knew teens did dumb things with their phones, but I never would have guessed that Alex, who is a sweet girl, would find herself in a situation like this. I wasn't sure if it was a crime, but I was pretty sure it was some kind of harassment and she needed to report it."

Dena met with the girls that afternoon, and Alex broke down sobbing when Dena told her she needed to report what was happening.

"She didn't want her parents to know, and she definitely didn't want to talk to the police about any of it," Dena says. "She was so embarrassed that she was actually considering going out with the boy to appease him. I felt so angry at the boy and so bad for her."

Dena prayed hard about what to do next.

"I asked God what I should do, and the answer was very

clear to me. I needed to help Alex speak for herself. I did not think I should do the speaking for her, though I was willing if she needed me to. I thought she needed to know that she could speak the truth and that boy could not control her."

It took a lot of coaxing over the course of a few days, but eventually Dena convinced Alex to tell her parents and the school principal about what was happening. The principal handled the situation immediately, bringing in the boy's parents and alerting the police, who confiscated the phone and photos. In the end, no charges were filed, but the teens involved learned a painful lesson.

It was as happy an ending as Dena could have hoped for, but still she was left feeling sad.

"You know what broke my heart the most about all of this?" she says. "It was that Alex felt she could not stand up for herself. That because she had made a mistake, this boy had power over her and she could not tell anyone."

But Dena knew better than that. Using her motherly instincts and a strong sense of justice, she encouraged a frightened young girl to stand up against abuse and speak the truth.

"I know she was scared, but I'm proud of Alex," Dena says. "I'm glad I could be there to help her speak up. We all make mistakes, but we can't let them control us forever. Simply telling the truth can be very freeing."

THE PRIVILEGE OF SEEING

Jesus made his presence known to Elizabeth, Anna, and Mary Magdalene. Time and again, we see that when Jesus makes his presence known, the fruit of that encounter is a desire to share the Good News with others. Elizabeth exclaimed words we still recite today in the Hail Mary. Anna was quietly rewarded for a lifetime of faithfulness in the temple and then lived out her remaining years telling others about the child Jesus. Mary Magdalene saw the horrors of Jesus' passion and death, but then was first to taste the sweetness of Easter joy, and she ran to tell the others what she had seen.

Jesus speaks to us and connects with us through our humanity, and part of every woman's humanity is her feminine gift of nurturing love. There truly are things in this world that only a mother could love, because we women have been gifted with a special capacity for generosity and self-giving love. What's more, we are natural relationship builders. We see and hear small details and understand feelings that are sometimes lost on others. We readily speak the language of emotions, noticing and caring about how every little thing affects others, especially those we live and work with.

Jesus appeals to our womanly nature when, as he did for Elizabeth and Anna, he comes to us as a baby. Babies know no boundaries. With sweetness and innocence, they dive into our arms and demand that we notice them and take care of them.

I recently offered to hold a friend's baby for her at a family party. She readily handed me her sweet, drooling bundle of a daughter, and the baby girl immediately lunged for my earrings. She wet my neck with sloppy kisses, patted my cheeks with chubby hands, and then spat up her lunch on my shoulder. I was charmed. No, really I was. There is something about babies that makes us want to connect with them and love them, no matter what it might cost us.

Jesus wants that kind of connection with each of us; he longs for it with you right now. Take a moment to consider the ways in which Jesus might make his presence known to you, the quiet ways he might come to you, small and defenseless as a human baby.

Where can you find Jesus in the world today? Beneath what kinds of human suffering might he be hidden? In what helpless human beings might you sense his presence? And then, when you find him, how will you follow in your biblical sisters' footsteps and use your voice to acknowledge his presence, his love, and his triumph over death?

Jesus, you gave women the special privilege of seeing you and knowing you before anyone else. Help me to see the ways in which you come to me each day, quiet and small, like a tiny baby. Help me to see you in others who are suffering. Help me to know the ways you want to connect with me. Give me a voice. I want to tell you everything I think and feel. I want to be heard. Amen.

CHAPTER 6

YOU ARE FULFILLED

"Look at the birds of the air: they neither sow nor reap
nor gather into barns, and yet your heavenly Father
feeds them. Are you not of more value than they?"

(MATTHEW 6:26)

One of my favorite characters in the popular movie *O Brother, Where Art Thou?* is Penny, the wife of the main character, Everett McGill. Everett, played by George Clooney, has been sent to prison, leaving Penny with seven young daughters to raise alone during the Depression. Throughout the movie, we hear Penny refer to the new man she plans to marry during Everett's absence as "bona fide," meaning that he has a good job and earns a decent living. Jobless and penniless, poor Everett is not bona fide at all.

Though her personality is exaggerated, I think Penny is a character women everywhere can understand. Who doesn't want a "bona fide" man? Having a man provide for us is an especially feminine way of experiencing love. Even those of us who earn our own money, own our own homes, and pay our own bills desire a man who takes responsibility and will take care of us. It's built into our female DNA. This desire is not weakness or neediness, but a natural way women in particular experience the feeling of being loved.

I once saw a young woman wearing a T-shirt that read, girls just wanna have FUNDS. Funny, but kind of accurate, too. Of course gold-digging, selfishness, and greed represent a natural feminine inclination gone awry in sinful ways, but at the heart of the jokes, in movies or on T-shirts, is something real. Women crave security, both emotional and physical. We have needs, and we want a man to meet them. Real-world circumstances and relationships, however, with their real-world faults and failures, frequently disappoint us.

JESUS IS BONA FIDE

Only Jesus does not disappoint. He's bona fide. He wants to meet your needs, and he has an endless capacity to fulfill all of them.

Now, you might be thinking, "He wants to meet all of my needs? Oh sure, right. I can't afford my mortgage, my boss is a total jerk, my best friend has breast cancer, my husband and I aren't getting along, my daughter was caught smoking at school . . . I have no idea where Jesus is in all of this!"

Your details might be different, but we all know that life can be a real mess sometimes. Some of the messes are of our own making, but many of them are not.

"Every single day, I'm a victim," a girlfriend once complained to me. "I wake up in the morning, see what happens, and then react to all the problems that come my way."

Do you ever feel that way? I think every one of us can relate to the feelings my friend expressed, but that's no way to live. Where is Jesus when life gets miserable and messy? Would you believe me if I told you he's right there next to you in the mess, wanting to help you and meet your every need? He's only waiting for you to turn to him and trust him.

Some of the most inspiring women we meet in the stories of the Bible are those who trusted Jesus with all they had. They sacrificed all they had to give, placing their physical and emotional needs in his hands, and they were rewarded for that trust.

HE ONLY WANTS EVERYTHING

Let's begin with the generous widow Jesus praised in the Gospel of Luke. Hers is a small, seemingly insignificant story, but as we have learned, there are no insignificant details in the life and words of Jesus.

> He looked up and saw the rich putting their gifts into
> the treasury; and he saw a poor widow put in two cop-
> per coins. And he said, "Truly I tell you, this poor widow
> has put in more than all of them; for they all contributed

out of their abundance, but she out of her poverty put in
all the living that she had." (Luke 21:1–4)

Can you imagine the kind of trust it would take to make a
contribution of all you have? How many of us make contribu-
tions, financially or otherwise, "from our poverty"?

I once received an unexpected check and immediately felt
inspired to give the entire amount to someone I knew who
was in need. Somewhere along the way, though, between
cashing the check and putting the money into an envelope to
give away, I second-guessed my plan.

The person I planned to give the money to would appre-
ciate a donation in any amount, I thought to myself. Besides,
what would my husband say? Our family budget doesn't have
a lot of wiggle room. Shouldn't I hold on to at least part of the
money, in case we needed it for some unexpected expense in
the future? What if we had an emergency car repair or medical bill?

By worldly standards, my hesitation might have seemed
quite reasonable, but truthfully, my thought process demonstrated a remarkable lack of trust in Jesus. I was holding on to
my precious coins, refusing to give, even from my "excess."

We are such silly humans sometimes. How patiently Jesus
reminds us, time and time again, that he will provide for our
every need, and yet still we refuse to place our trust in him.
Instead, we trust in our jobs, our bank accounts, our human
relationships, and our own skills, abilities, and accomplish-

ments, despite the fact that these things never fail to disappoint us.

Like I said, silly humans.

TRUST COMES FIRST

How many tears have we shed, how many hours of sleep have we lost worrying about making money, saving money, and all the things we need to buy with money, for ourselves and our families? I'm right there with you, too often lying awake at night wondering and worrying about the future. The kids need new sneakers again. How will we ever afford college? How much of that dental bill will the insurance cover?

And yet Jesus tells us so clearly not to worry, that God will provide for our every need:

> "Therefore I tell you, do not be anxious about your life, what you shall eat or what you shall drink, nor about your body, what you shall put on. Is not life more than food, and the body more than clothing? Look at the birds of the air: they neither sow nor reap nor gather into barns, and yet your heavenly Father feeds them. Are you not of more value than they? . . . Therefore do not be anxious, saying, 'What shall we eat?' or 'What shall we drink?' or 'What shall we wear?' For the Gentiles seek all these things; and your heavenly Father knows that you

need them all. But seek first his kingdom and his righ-
teousness, and all these things shall be yours as well."
(Matthew 6:25–26; 31–33)

These are such comforting words, if only we will listen to
them. And not only listen to them, but accept them into our
hearts. Surely the widow who gave away her last two coins
knew and accepted God's promise to provide for her. She,
who had so little, gave all of it away, demonstrating exactly
the kind of trust that Jesus longs for each of us to place in him.

Will you cling to your bank account, or to Jesus? Will you
seek a "bona fide" man who will meet some of your needs, or
will you seek Jesus, who will meet all of your needs?

Think of how scary it would be to plunk your last two
coins into a basket. It's frightening sometimes to think of what
exactly Jesus is asking of us. He doesn't want just some small
part of us; he wants all of us. Every bit of us. He doesn't want
some fraction of what we have; he wants all that we have. He
doesn't want five minutes of your time. He wants all of your
time. Your whole life. And to show us that he means it, he sets
a dramatic example of self-giving love for each of us.

Do you have a crucifix, at home or in your church? Take
a look at it. Not in the way that we look at everyday things
without really seeing them. Really look at it. Look at him.
Look at Jesus' broken body as he hangs there, bleeding. Does
this look like the kind of guy who wants to give you just one
small part of himself? Does this look like the kind of man who

wants to give you just five minutes of his time? Does this look like a man who will fail to love you completely?

Of course not.

Jesus looks like the kind of man, the kind of God, who wants to give you all that he has and to provide for your every need, despite great suffering and even at the cost of his very life. He is only waiting for you to trust him enough and to let go of your trust in lesser things enough to receive him.

POURING IT ALL OUT

In the Gospel stories, there are two very similar stories of women who anoint Jesus with costly oil. In Luke, we meet a woman who was a repentant sinner. She found Jesus where he was having dinner, at the home of Simon, a Pharisee, and she ran to him.

> And behold, a woman of the city, who was a sinner, when she learned that he was sitting at table in the Pharisee's house, brought an alabaster flask of ointment, and standing behind him at his feet, weeping, she began to wet his feet with her tears, and wiped them with the hair of her head, and kissed his feet, and anointed them with the ointment. (Luke 7:37–38)

What stands out to you in this passage? I am always struck by the intimacy described here. The woman wept, covering Jesus' feet with her tears, and then she kissed his feet and wiped them with her hair. *With her hair.* Here was a woman who held nothing back. With complete and total trust, she threw herself at Jesus' feet, trusting in his mercy, goodness, and love. She did not care about others present in the room, what her actions might have looked like, or what people might have thought. Though this woman did not have much, she poured out all that she had at Jesus' feet: contrition, love, ointment, tears, and her hair.

Not surprisingly, Simon didn't understand the woman's actions. He expressed disgust at the fact that Jesus allowed a "sinful" woman to touch him. But Jesus understood. He was moved by the woman's display of repentance, trust, and love.

Then turning toward the woman he said to Simon, "Do you see this woman? I entered your house, you gave me no water for my feet, but she has wet my feet with her tears and wiped them with her hair. You gave me no kiss, but from the time I came in she has not ceased to kiss my feet. You did not anoint my head with oil, but she has anointed my feet with ointment. Therefore I tell you, her sins, which are many, are forgiven, for she loved much; but he who is forgiven little, loves little." (Luke 7:44–47)

She presented her very self to Jesus with great humility and love. She brought to him the only things that she had and remained at his feet, sinful and sorrowful. She worshipped him, loved him, and honored him with the only things she had. Consequently, Jesus loved her and accepted her as she was and gave her the gift of forgiveness.

We don't all need to bathe Jesus' feet with our tears to find forgiveness, but this story is a beautiful example of the kind of trust Jesus wants from us, especially when we have sinned. He wants us to throw ourselves upon him, trusting in his goodness and love with abandon; he wants to meet all of our needs.

Sin is a debt. Whether that debt is large or small, none of us are able to repay it on our own, and that is why we need Jesus. We need a God at whose feet we can fall, trusting in him to pay our debts, forgive our sins, and give us a new life.

The point that Jesus made to the men who would judge the repentant woman in this story is an important one. He referred to her sins as "many" and explained that when she repented, she showed "great love." We are all sinners, and sometimes the weight of our sinfulness can overwhelm us. Even those of us who have reformed our lives sometimes have past sins that haunt us. Perhaps there is something dark from your past that lurks in the background of your heart, making you feel unworthy of God's love. In this passage, Jesus speaks a hope-filled message directly to the heart of every sinner. Those who have greatly sinned are uniquely capable of great love.

BREAKING OUR JARS

Another story took place in Bethany, shortly before Jesus' passion and death. This time the woman was Mary, the sister of Martha and Lazarus—someone we already know had great love for and trust in Jesus. "And while he was at Bethany in the house of Simon the leper, as he sat at table, a woman came with an alabaster jar of ointment of pure nard, very costly, and she broke the jar and poured it over his head" (Mark 14:3).

In this story Mary arrived with a jar containing expensive perfumed oil. She broke the jar and poured all of the ointment on Jesus' head. Mary's actions held nothing back; she was "all in." There could be no un-breaking of the jar, no way to retrieve the precious ointment, and so in this way she demonstrated a profound love for Jesus. She trusted him completely and wanted to give him everything, without holding anything back.

Here again, as in the previous story of anointing, some of those present objected to such a lavish display: "But there were some who said to themselves indignantly, 'Why was the ointment thus wasted? For this ointment might have been sold for more than three hundred denarii, and given to the poor.' And they reproached her" (Mark 14:4–5).

But once again, Jesus affirmed the goodness of the woman's demonstration of trust and love: "But Jesus said, 'Let her alone; why do you trouble her? She has done a beautiful thing to me. For you always have the poor with you, and whenever you will, you can do good to them; but you will not always have me. She has done what she could; she has anointed my body beforehand for burying. And truly, I say to you, wherever the gospel is preached in the whole world, what she has done will be told in memory of her'" (Mark 14:6–9).

Are you holding on to and protecting an alabaster jar out of fear and insecurity? What is preventing you from trusting Jesus, breaking open your jar, and pouring out all that you have?

IN PERSON
HEARING GOD'S VOICE

As a teenager, when Anne went away one summer to volunteer at a summer camp run by the Missionaries of Charity (Mother Teresa's nuns), she was not expecting to have a life-changing encounter with Jesus. But her mother had other ideas.

"She said to me, 'I want you to go away and fall in love with Jesus,'" Anne laughs now, more than twenty years later. "I mean, how corny can you get?"

But at camp, led by the sisters and following a strict schedule of prayer times and work, Anne did have a spiritual reawakening.

"I didn't exactly 'fall in love with Jesus,'" she says, "but I did come to know and love my faith in a way I hadn't before. I never really had a 'falling out' with my faith, but I never really had a passion for it, either, before that time. We all need to come to a point when we decide to make our faith our own, and that summer, I did that."

The priest who said daily Mass for the sisters and the volunteers had a remarkable devotion to the Eucharist, and it was through receiving the Eucharist that Anne felt herself drawn closer and closer to Jesus. "When Father said Mass, I really felt that he could see Jesus present there in the Eucharist. Because of that, Jesus became real to me, instead of a distant figure," she says.

The sisters Anne met also had a profound effect on her blossoming spiritual life. "I had known other sisters before who were not very personable and almost did not seem like real people," she recalls, "but the sisters at the camp were so accessible. They were really and truly joyful. When I spent time with them, I came away thinking that I wanted whatever it was that they had. Of course, Jesus is what they had."

Anne went on to volunteer at that camp for many more summers before getting married and becoming a mom to four young children. She still benefits from the spiritual lessons and habits she cultivated with the sisters, especially the habit of listening to God.

"There have been times in my life when I've become very aware of God's guidance," she says. "I never heard voices from the sky or anything, but I would feel confident that God was looking out for me and listening to my prayers. I realize now that nothing changed for me to feel that way. Those opportunities were always there. He was always there, doing that, listening to me and speaking to me, but I needed to stop and listen. God talks to all of us. But the world is so noisy sometimes, we just don't hear."

Jesus, Anne has learned, can speak to us anytime, anywhere—even in the midst of the busyness of our everyday lives.

"I am sometimes struck by the tiniest detail of something and feel the presence of Jesus right there with me," she shares. "It's like he is letting me know that he can speak to me right where I am, if I will just listen. If we are looking, we will find him, right where we are."

EASIER PRAYED THAN DONE

Do you pray the Our Father? I think the words "Thy will be done" are some of the scariest ones Jesus ever asked us to pray. I remember once, when praying for a friend's baby who was very sick, I could not bring myself to pray those words on her behalf.

"Thy will be done"? What if God's will is not what we want?

The kind of trust Jesus asks us to have in his goodness is simple, but it's not easy. No matter how many times he reminds us that he loves us and wants to provide for our every need, still we withhold our trust. Out of human frailty and shortsightedness, we cling to lesser things. We place our trust in people and things that always fall short of the kind of love and security we seek.

Look again at Jesus hanging on the cross. Will you believe now that he loves you? Will you trust him?

What is standing in the way of you dropping all of your coins into the basket or breaking open your jar of oil at Jesus' feet? Are you worried about what others might think? Are you afraid of suffering? Are you too attached to things or even people to place them in God's hands? Do you feel somehow unworthy of God's mercy and love?

Whatever obstacle stands in your way, reflect on it now. Imagine yourself standing in the presence of Jesus with all the barriers you have envisioned between you and him. There might be just one thing in the way, or maybe you have a pile of stuff that reaches to the ceiling. It doesn't matter. Give it all to Jesus. Ask him to remove whatever is keeping you from trusting him, praying these words:

> *Jesus, here are the things I am holding on to and hiding away out of fear. I believe, but my faith needs the strengthening that can only come from you. I hear your words of love and generosity in my ears, but I want to hold them in my heart. Take these things. Take all that I have until I am left with only you to cling to. And then*

help me, Jesus. Give me everything I need, as you promised you would. Help me to pray these words and mean them, without holding anything back. Amen.

Trust that Jesus hears your prayer and will answer it. He will give you all you need—and more.

CHAPTER 7

YOU ARE NURTURED

"When Jesus saw his mother, and the disciple whom he loved standing near, he said to his mother, 'Woman, behold, your son!' Then he said to the disciple, 'Behold, your mother!' And from that hour the disciple took her to his own home."

(JOHN 19:26–27)

I yelled at Mary once. Yes, that Mary—the Blessed Mother, our mother in heaven, whom we are supposed to love, emulate, cherish, and respect. I yelled at her.

I can explain. Sort of. The previous spring, the boarding school where my husband had taught math and science for nineteen years closed its doors, and he found himself without work. Despite this challenge, I tried my best to trust. I had recently done some reading about Mary and gained a greater appreciation for her role in our Church, so when months went by with no leads, I resisted the temptation to despair. I made a conscious choice to trust that Jesus, through Mary, would provide a new job for Dan.

I prayed hard to Mary, every day, with a positive and

confident attitude. I did all the things you are supposed to do: I prayed Rosaries and chaplets; I spent extra hours in the church. And it worked! During those weeks of prayer, I heard about a job opportunity at a new school and became convinced that this was the answer. I kept praying as I pushed my husband through the application process, and ultimately he was successful. He got the job! My prayers were answered!

But my joy didn't last. My husband gave his all to that job, working ridiculously long hours throughout the summer and early fall, but in the end, through a series of underhanded and unjust events, and through no fault of his own, he lost his job—the very job that Mary and I had picked out for him!

I was furious—with the unethical way things were handled at the school, for sure, but even more so with Mary. How dare she! How dare she take all my prayers and answer them with this gigantic mess! And that was when I yelled. I went to pray, and found myself yelling things at her in my mind instead, like "How could you?" and "Why did you?" and "What the heck?"

What the heck, indeed.

BE CAREFUL WHAT YOU PRAY FOR

I took a break from praying to Mary. It took me an angry little while, but eventually a small thought came to mind when I thought about Mary, our mother in heaven. Maybe the problem wasn't so much that she had let me down as that she had actually *answered* my prayer—my persistent, insistent, oh-so-specific prayer that she ask Jesus to provide this exact job for my husband. It obviously wasn't the right job for him, and I finally had to admit that Mary hadn't picked it. I had.

I was complaining to a close friend about all of this when she said to me, "It only looks and feels like God didn't come through. One thing I have learned is not to write the script as I pray. I think of the best answers to prayers; he tends to edit my screenplay with a heavy hand."

Wise words, and I am sometimes afraid to admit just how true they are. I don't know about you, but when I write out an amazing screenplay for my life, I don't want anyone editing it—not even God, and definitely not Mary.

Many of us have complicated relationships with our own mothers, so why should a relationship with our heavenly mother be any different? Perhaps you have never prayed to Mary, or perhaps you haven't ever fully understood what your relationship with her is meant to be. Some women suffer feelings of insecurity, anger, or resentment when Mary is held up as the perfect woman and perfect mother—it just seems to highlight their personal failures. And let's face it: We all have failures.

Especially when it comes to womanhood and motherhood, those very things Mary supposedly models perfectly, we fail hundreds of times a day. We make wrong decisions about our bodies, about sex, and about pregnancy. When we have children, we grow tired of and lose patience with them while they are small; we make the wrong choices and fail to control them when they are older; and we can spend whole lifetimes of regret when our children grow up, make bad choices, and don't turn out the way we think they should have.

HOW CAN WE RELATE TO A PERFECT WOMAN?

In the face of our own shortcomings, having someone tell us to turn to Mary, the perfect woman and perfect mother, with all of our sorrows and failures can feel like an insult. Just what makes Mary our mother, anyway, and what exactly does that mean?

Well, let's go back to when Jesus gave us Mary as our mother. It was when he hung, bleeding, on the cross, giving his very life for our salvation, because he loved each of us just that much. "When Jesus saw his mother, and the disciple whom he loved standing near, he said to his mother, 'Woman, behold, your son!' Then he said to the disciple, 'Behold, your mother!' And from that hour the disciple took her to his own home" (John 19:26–27).

Let's be clear about what is going on here. Jesus gave Mary to John so John would care for her when Jesus was gone, but he also gave John to Mary, so she could care for him. And in this instance, John stands for every one of us. Jesus gave every one of us Mary to be our mother.

Why is this significant? Because Mary was so very precious to Jesus in the first place. He loves us so much that he wants us to have every good thing, and his mother was one of the very best things Jesus had.

A GOOD MOTHER IS A PRECIOUS GIFT

Think of the gift of a good mother! Whether or not it is lived out perfectly, the calling of motherhood is a high one. Those of us who are mothers know all too well the challenges of living out this calling, but Mary was the perfect example of a mother—a role that is naturally meant to be generous, nurturing, self-giving, and full of love. Mary lived out those things perfectly with her son, and now Jesus wants to give us the same thing: a loving relationship with his mother.

Do you have that kind of relationship with Jesus' mother? Because of the limitations of our human understanding, many of us put up barriers to a relationship with Mary. We have mothers on earth; why do we need one in heaven? Well, perhaps it's not so much that we *need* Mary, but that Mary is such a beautiful gift to us that we should care about what we miss when we don't recognize her as our mother.

Think of a time in your life when you felt nurtured and mothered by someone. It might have been your own mother, or it might have been a sister, grandmother, aunt, or friend. We all have had times in our lives when we needed care—physical, emotional, or spiritual care—and those needs were met beautifully by the loving care of a woman God placed in our lives.

Mary wants to play that loving, nurturing, generous role in our lives every day. She loves us and cares for us whether we recognize her or not, but think of how we might be spiritually and emotionally fed by engaging in a maternal relationship with Mary.

MOTHERS ARE INTERCESSORS

Mothers play such a special role in families. One of the most important things a good mother brings to her children is softness and sensitivity to their needs. My kids recognize that I play this role in our family, and they come to me with all kinds of needs.

If you are a mother, you know what I'm talking about. If kids want anything—from a new bike or pizza for dinner to extra time to watch TV—they go to Mom first. She's their best bet. They might whine, complain, nag, and interrupt her a thousand times a day, but they never fail to go to her first. They instinctively know a mom cares about her kids' every need and desire and will do whatever she can to fulfill them. This is true whether she is able to provide what they need herself or must seek out someone else who can help them. In my house, the kids often come to me first, even when what they want comes from their father. They know I have a special hold on his attention; they know he listens to me and wants to please me, and therefore I can intercede on their behalf.

We understand these kinds of relationships on a human level. If we sometimes freeze at the daunting idea of having a perfect mother in heaven, it can help to remember that our relationship with Mary is meant to be very much like a good mother-child relationship here on earth. We can "nag" her with all our wants and needs, and she will listen lovingly and then do everything she can to take care of us.

Imagine for a moment that you have an "in" with a very important and powerful person. Perhaps a prominent businessman or a popular movie star or an influential world leader has a personal, special kind of affection for you. This individual loves you so much that he or she would do anything for you. Well, Mary is that person. She is more important and more powerful than any human on earth could ever be, and you have an "in" with her. Jesus gave her to you as your mother, and she wants to give you every good thing. We can always ask Mary for the things we desire; we can always turn to her for nurturing love, and she will always bring us to Jesus.

How does this work? People sometimes object to the idea of praying to Mary. They see Catholic devotions to her as a kind of idol worship. But when we reverence Mary, we do not idolize her. She is not a god, but she is a perfect human being whom God himself loved and respected when he walked the earth. When we pray to Mary, we don't worship her; instead we ask her to intercede for us, and she never fails to draw us closer to Jesus.

MARY IS A "KEEPER"

One of my favorite passages in the Gospel is the one that describes Mary when Jesus was born.

> And they went with haste, and found Mary and Joseph, and the babe lying in a manger. And when they saw it they made known the saying which had been told them concerning this child; and all who heard it wondered at what the shepherds told them. But Mary kept all these things, pondering them in her heart. (Luke 2:16–19)

Do you see the profound lesson Mary teaches us here, without even saying a word? She had just given birth to the Savior of the world. She was holding Jesus—God made man—in her arms. And what did she say? Nothing. What did she do? Nothing.

Imagine if an event of this proportion happened to you today. I don't know about you, but if I were taking part in one of the most significant events in the history of humankind, I would probably be freaking out just a little bit. I would be preparing myself to speak on the matter, answer some questions, and quite possibly tidy up the manger scene a bit before the press arrived.

But Mary did not run around giving interviews and offering eggnog to the shepherds. She held that baby boy, she "kept all these things," and she "ponder[ed] them in her heart." She knew the value of the bond she was creating with her newborn son. Women know the bond of motherhood intuitively. Even those of us who have never raised children of our own have a natural gift for creating bonds through human relationships. We excel at the language of communion and relational love. Mary's example in the story of Jesus' birth shows us the value of the mother-child relationship as it mirrors the intimate love and communion God wants to have with each one of us.

ALLOW YOURSELF TO BE NURTURED

We women are tough. We can handle pretty much anything the world might throw at us, from marital challenges and health issues to parenting trials and financial difficulties. We can tame a toddler tantrum with one hand while whipping up dinner for six from a can of soup and a box of macaroni with the other. Our strength is a wonderful gift, for ourselves, our families, and the world at large. We sometimes get so used to "handling" things, though, that we forget our own need to be nurtured. Or maybe we reject the idea because it feels like weakness.

Do you need a mom? I do.

Thankfully, God has blessed me with a beautiful, loving mom here on earth and all kinds of generous women in my life who can play a motherly role when I need them to, but every one of us needs even more than that. We all hunger for the kind of super-mothering that comes from our super mother in heaven. We all long for the kind of nurturing, motherly love that can only come from Mary. Will you admit that you need it? Will you accept it?

BEING VULNERABLE

One of the greatest gifts that comes from fostering a relationship with Mary and accepting her motherly love is the opportunity to make ourselves spiritually and emotionally vulnerable. Many of us, and especially those of us who carry emotional wounds from our past, balk at the idea of being vulnerable. We build up tough exteriors as a means of making ourselves appear stronger than we really are inside.

I will never forget the first time I was in a car accident. I was a teenager at the time, a new and nervous driver, and the accident was entirely my fault. Thankfully no one was hurt, and I remember keeping my cool through the entire process that followed. I spoke to the other driver and we exchanged insurance information; when a police officer arrived, I answered his questions calmly. But then it was time to call home. I dialed the number and waited while it rang.

My mother answered the phone. The moment I heard her voice on the line, I fell apart. The cool, calm, businesslike teen was nowhere to be found. I was a blubbering mess on the phone.

"M-m-m-mooooom? I was in a car accident!" I managed to blurt out before collapsing in a heap of sobs.

My poor mother! I'm sure she thought I was hurt or that something much more tragic had happened than a fender bender in the parking lot.

I think my emotional response to hearing my mother's voice was telling, though. With my mom, I could let down my guard. It was OK to be honest about how I was feeling. It was OK to be vulnerable.

Vulnerability is not a popular attribute these days. Our culture tells us we need to be strong, tough, resilient, and independent. But deep inside, every one of us is truly vulnerable. Every one of us has doubts and weaknesses, worries and insecurities, even if we are afraid to let them show. It can be a great gift to have someone with whom we can safely be ourselves, with whom we can allow ourselves to be vulnerable— and every one of us has that person in Mary.

We can't heal wounds if we won't admit they are there.

What wounds do you have that might need healing, with Mary's help? Are there sins from your past that still haunt you? Guilty secrets you don't feel you can share with anyone else? Perhaps you harbor anger over a loss or how your life has not gone the way you planned. Bring these things to Mary. Bring anything to Mary. Pour out your heart to your mother in heaven, and she will look at you with her loving eyes and then show you how to find healing in Jesus, her Son.

MARY BRINGS US TO JESUS

The special, loving bond that Jesus and Mary share is especially apparent in the Gospel story of the Wedding at Cana. Here we find it is at Mary's request that Jesus performed the first miracle of his public life, by turning water into wine.

> On the third day there was a marriage at Cana in Galilee, and the mother of Jesus was there; Jesus also was invited to the marriage, with his disciples. When the wine failed, the mother of Jesus said to him, "They have no wine." And Jesus said to her, "O woman, what have you to do with me? My hour has not yet come." His mother said to the servants, "Do whatever he tells you." (John 2:1–5)

Without exchanging another word with his mother, Jesus

told the servers to fill some stone jars with water and then miraculously he changed the water into wine. And not just any wine—a wine that the head steward pronounced a very "good wine."

When I was younger, I used to be scandalized a bit by Jesus' reference to Mary as "woman" in this passage. To modern ears, it might sound disrespectful for a man to call his mother "woman," but Jesus' use of this word was actually very respectful. He used the word *woman* to highlight the beautiful womanly role Mary played in that moment. She was worried that the wedding hosts would be embarrassed. Mary responded as a woman—someone who pays attention to the small details and needs of others and cares deeply about their feelings. And then Mary acted as a woman—someone who can find ways to meet the needs of others, even if she is unable to meet them herself. Confident in her son's love and loyalty, she instructed the waiters to do whatever Jesus told them.

And that's the same message Mary has for us today: Do whatever Jesus tells you. She always leads us to Jesus, and we can learn from her confident trust in his power and goodness. We can learn from her faithful example of nurturing love and caring for the hosts of the wedding, even about a seemingly insignificant detail, like running out of wine. But what I think we should learn most is that Mary is a loving mother. She cares about all the little things of our lives and how those things make us feel. She sees us with the loving eyes of a mother who only wants the very best for us. She longs to help us grow closer to Jesus and have the kind of loving closeness she shares with him. She knows that only he can free us from our burdens, cleanse us of our sins, and give us lasting joy.

IN PERSON
FINDING MARY THROUGH SUFFERING

Michelle was raised Catholic, but she did not grow up knowing much about Mary. "I guess I heard about the Rosary sometimes, but that was it," she says. "We went to Mass, but we never talked about Mary at home or anything. She was one of the figures in our nativity set at Christmas each year, and that was about it."

After graduating from college and beginning her first "real" job as an accountant, she married a more serious Catholic, and it was her husband, Ben, who first introduced her to Mary.

"I thought it was kind of weird, to be honest with you," she recalls. "I prayed to God, I prayed to Jesus, but who was Mary, anyway? She was just a person, like me. Why would I go to her when I could just go to God?"

Ben had a real devotion to Mary, though, and he encouraged his wife to pray to her. "I would say the Rosary with him, to make him happy," Michelle says, "but it never really felt like a big deal to me. The first time I ever actually felt like I needed Mary was when my own mom died."

Losing her mother at a young age to pancreatic cancer was life changing for Michelle. She was newly pregnant with her first child at the time, and found herself without the motherly support so many of her friends had as they adjusted to married life and motherhood.

"When she was healthy, I definitely took my mom for granted," says Michelle. "She wasn't perfect, of course, but she was my mom! She was there for me. She always loved me and looked out for me. She would have been an awesome grandma, but I never thought much about those things until she got sick."

Her mother's illness progressed so quickly that Michelle felt stunned after she died. One day, months after her mother's death, she was at Mass and was surprised to find herself suddenly crying.

"I was praying, asking God to help me be a good mother to my own new baby, when it suddenly occurred to me that I had no mother to show me how to be a good mom. I felt so helpless and scared, I just started crying."

It was in that moment that she felt the loving presence of Jesus. "It honestly felt like he just wrapped his arms around me with such love that I stopped crying. I looked up, and there was Mary, looking at me."

It was the statue of Mary at the front of Michelle's church, decorated with fresh flowers for Mother's Day. In that emotional moment, Michelle felt Jesus' loving gift of his mother, Mary.

"She was so beautiful and so welcoming that I started crying again. But this time it was because I knew I had a mother, not because I lost one."

In the years since that day, Michelle has gone on to have two more children, and she says her own motherhood has forced her to lean even harder on her relationship with Mary at times.

"Especially during times when the kids are sick or misbehaving, I find myself wondering what Mary would do. I pour my heart out to her, and she always listens. Mary knows about pain, especially in motherhood. I think of how she lost Jesus and how I lost my mom, and I feel more bonded to her than ever. I think she looks out for me, just like my own mom would if she were here."

COME TO MAMA

Many of the prayers we say to Mary are repetitive ones. We repeat the words of the angel Gabriel in the Hail Mary, and we repeat dozens of Hail Marys every time we pray the Rosary.

"Hail Mary, hail Mary, hail Mary . . ."

To an outsider, it's easy to see how this might seem weird or even childish. I prefer the word *childlike* to describe our prayers to Mary. We come to her as little children, and she responds to us as a mother does. "Mama, mama, mama!" we cry, pulling at the hem of her skirt and asking for her attention, and just as mothers on earth respond to their children's cries, she never fails to answer us. She leans in close to listen, wraps us in her protective arms, and shows us how to bring all of our cares to Jesus.

If you have never prayed to Mary, or if you haven't in a while, there is no time like right now. Pray with me now and trust that Jesus' gift of his mother will bear good fruit in your life.

Mary, I don't always remember to call on you. Just like children on earth take their mothers' love and caring for granted, I sometimes do that with you. But Jesus, as he hung dying for my sins, gave you to me as a precious gift, and he gave me to you. I trust that Jesus wanted you to be my mother, and so I turn to you now. I fall into your arms and let go. I let go of all the world's pretenses, all my worries and fears, and all that stands in the way of growing in love for Jesus through you. I am afraid even to admit that I am afraid, but you see me as I am and love me as only a mother can. See me as your little child, pick me up with love, and bring me to Jesus, because we know he will give me everything I need. Amen.

Mary hears you. And she is smiling.

YOU ARE WORTH IT

Have you ever seen a person holding up a sign reading john 3:16 in the stands at a crowded sports event? Even people with no knowledge of the Bible will usually recognize the citation of this one verse. Do you know what the words are?

> For God so loved the world that he gave his only Son, so that everyone who believes in him might not perish but might have eternal life.

You might be familiar with these words, but have you actually heard them? I mean really *heard* them, with your heart? Through these words, God tells us that what we are about to hear is a love story. The story of Jesus' birth, life, death, and resurrection is the greatest love story of all time—and you are in it.

Jesus did not come to the world to save some faceless, nameless throng of human beings; he did not come because he cared about "humanity" in some generic way. He came because he loves *you*. He knows you and loves you with a unique and infinite love. You are the reason he was born, walked the earth, spoke to crowds, performed miracles, and gave himself up to die, bleeding, on a cross. You are the reason he rose from the dead. You are the reason he walked the earth, speaking words of hope, healing, and eternal life.

BECAUSE HE LOVES THE WORLD. BECAUSE HE LOVES YOU.

But Jesus does not walk the streets of our town today; instead we live in a world where it is easy to feel lost, broken, wounded, disappointed, empty, and sad. We can read a book like this one and want to open ourselves up to the ways Jesus wants to change our lives—but then life happens. We get busy and distracted. The love story of Jesus' life and the words he spoke when he was on earth can feel very long ago and far away.

And that is why we need to hear the rest of the Good News. It starts with love—that verse on a sign at a ballgame— but it does not end there. There is much we can learn from the real women who knew and touched and talked to Jesus thousands of years ago, but it's important to recognize that he is still with us. He did not leave us when he left the earth. He promised to stay.

"And lo, I am with you always, to the close of the age" (Matthew 28:20).

Before he ascended into heaven, Jesus established ways he could remain with us, ways he could continue to love, strengthen, help, heal, affirm, fulfill, and nurture us. He blesses us in very real ways, with very tangible graces, through the sacraments of the Church. I am going to mention just two of them briefly here, but I hope you will be encouraged enough to explore them more on your own.

FIND HEALING IN CONFESSION

Confession? Oh, ugh. Why do we have to talk about this? you might be thinking.

Maybe you have never been to confession.

Or maybe confession was something you did in second grade. It was weird and scary and made you feel bad about yourself. You have no desire to do that again.

Or maybe you used to go to confession, but it's been so long now, you are afraid to go back. You can open your heart to Jesus in private, but saying your sins out loud to a priest is more than you can even think about doing right now.

Or maybe you do go to confession sometimes, but it feels kind of useless. You aren't really sure what it's supposed to do for you, or what you are supposed to get out of it.

It's OK to feel like this; these are very human feelings. I have experienced many of them myself. I procrastinate some-times before going to confession, even when I know I really need to go, even when I am aching and longing for forgive-ness, and even when I know how much Jesus loves me and wants to heal me. Still I am afraid and doubtful. I feel dirty, broken, and unworthy. I am like a sick person who avoids the doctor.

In confession, though, the priest is not the "doctor." Jesus is. When he appeared to his disciples after he rose from them dead, Jesus gave them the ability to stand in his place when forgiving sins. "Jesus said to them again, 'Peace be with you. As the Father has sent me, even so I send you.' And when he had said this, he breathed on them, and said to them, 'Receive the Holy Spirit. If you forgive the sins of any, they are forgiven; if you retain the sins of any, they are retained'" (John 20:21–23).

It is Jesus himself we meet in confession. Of course you can pray on your own and tell Jesus you are sorry for your sins, but confession is a very real way for you to encounter Jesus and experience the kind of peace, love, forgiveness, and healing that can only come from him.

I went to confession recently, and after I had confessed my sins, the priest asked me, "Which of the things you have just told me bothers you the most?" I mentioned one sin that bothered me, but I continued to think about his question afterward.

The thing that bothered me most was not any one thing at all; it was all the things. It was that I keep messing up my relationships, that I keep making selfish choices, and that I keep hurting myself and others with pride, anger, and grasping at fleeting pleasures, even when I know better. It was that not only am I not perfect, but I actively do bad things sometimes.

Confession is the place where we can bring those kinds of feelings—the ones that threaten to eat us up inside and destroy our happiness—and exchange them for Jesus' healing peace and love. We all want that. We all need that. Meeting Jesus in confession is the place to get it.

FIND STRENGTH IN THE EUCHARIST

The night before he died, Jesus was very sad. He was sad because he knew what was about to happen, but also because he knew that he would be leaving the ones he loved so much. This is why he gave us the Eucharist during that last meal he shared with his disciples. It was a way that he could stay with us, the ones he loves, even after he was gone.

"And he took bread, and when he had given thanks he broke it and gave it to them, saying, 'This is my body which is given for you. Do this in remembrance of me'" (Luke 22:19).

How meaningful is receiving the Eucharist for you? Many of us remember our first Communions, when we received the Eucharist for the first time, wearing a white dress and veil. Even if we were too distracted by parties and presents to focus on the gift we received that day, most of us have been receiving the Eucharist since.

But how often do we think about why Jesus gave us the

Eucharist? Why would he take on the form of bread and wine and invite us to eat it?

Again, it's because he loves us so much.

Love longs for connection and intimacy. Consider the love between friends, between a parent and child, or between a husband and wife. Each kind of love demands openness and the giving of oneself to the other in a personal and intimate way. Jesus loves us so much that it wasn't enough to give up his life on the cross for us. He wants to continue to give himself to us. He gives us his body, physically and spiritually, in a uniquely intimate way, through the Eucharist.

Just as our bodies need food for good health, so, too, our souls need food for good health. The Eucharist—Jesus himself—is the spiritual food our souls long for. In the Eucharist, Jesus comes to us simply, humbly, and without making demands. He comes to enter our bodies and our souls in a deeply intimate way. He comes to feed us with himself.

Are you hungry?

When our stomachs are empty, we are driven to find food and eat it, but it may not be quite so easy to recognize spiritual hunger. We may not know that the longing and emptiness we sometimes feel inside is a spiritual hunger, a healthy longing for God himself. We all have a yearning for something we were made for—a communion with Jesus—and we find that communion in the Eucharist.

AN INVITATION

I don't know why this book ended up in your hands, but God does. He knows the ways he wants to change your life and the plans he has for your happiness in this life and the next. He has big plans for your joy.

So much about our world today is empty and cold. If some of that emptiness and cold has seeped into your heart, I pray that this book has warmed you, just a bit, to the idea that you were made for something better, something bigger, and something new. You were made for an intimate relationship with a God who knows you and loves you inside and out. You were made for Jesus.

Jesus wants to bless you. He wants to love, strengthen, heal, affirm, hear, fulfill, and nurture you. All you have to do is ask him. So let go of everything that has been holding you back. Push fear out of the way and claim the peace, joy, and fulfillment that are yours.

Now is the time. Come to Jesus, and be loved. You're worth it!

ABOUT THE AUTHOR

Danielle Bean is publisher and editor-in-chief of *Catholic Digest*. She is the creator and host of *The Gist*, a weekly Catholic women's television talk show. The author of several books, she is a regular guest on Catholic radio and a popular speaker on various topics relating to marriage, motherhood, and family life.

NOTES

NOTES

Resisting Happiness
Matthew Kelly

Get a FREE* copy at **DynamicCatholic.com**.
Shipping and handling not included.

THE
DYNAMIC CATHOLIC
INSTITUTE

[MISSION]

To re-energize the Catholic Church in America by
developing world-class resources that inspire people to
rediscover the genius of Catholicism.

[VISION]

To be the innovative leader in the New Evangelization
helping Catholics and their parishes become
the-best-version-of-themselves

Join us in re-energizing the Catholic Church.
Become a Dynamic Catholic Ambassador today!

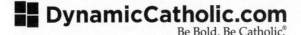

DynamicCatholic.com
Be Bold. Be Catholic.®

n